THE HOW AND WHY WONDER BOOK OF

MAGNETS
AND MAGNETISM

Written by
MARTIN L. KEEN

Illustrated by
GEORGE ZAFFO

Editorial Production:

Washington, D. C.

Children's Museum, Brooklyn, New York

Publishers • NEW YORK

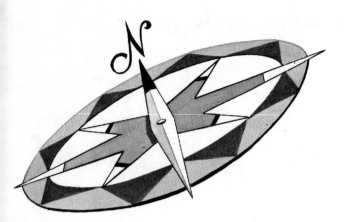

Introduction

Through the ages, magnetism has held a fascination for everyone. The allure of magnets continues to this day. Any boy or girl with a magnet will be engrossed with it for many an hour. And, if father and mother have a chance, they will experiment with it too. This *How and Why Wonder Book of Magnets and Magnetism* will help boys, girls, fathers, and mothers satisfy their curiosity about the mysterious force of magnetism.

It is very easy to find out what magnets will do, yet it is far from obvious what magnetism is. With the knowledge of what magnets do, scientists and inventors have developed hundreds of practical ways of using them in our homes and in industry.

In magnetism, we have an excellent example of a physical phenomenon that is useful even though much remains to be learned about it. Gravity is another such example. Both are puzzling but very useful forces. In each case, the challenge to scientists is to probe deeper and to learn more about them.

This *How and Why Wonder Book of Magnets and Magnetism* systematically summarizes much that is known about magnets. At the same time, it suggests that a great deal remains to be learned. Perhaps it will stimulate young readers to become partners of scientists in the never-ending search for knowledge. And that is the method of scientists — always investigating unknown questions, always seeking answers.

Paul E. Blackwood

Dr. Blackwood is a professional employee in the U. S. Office of Education. This book was edited by him in his private capacity and no official support or endorsement by the Office of Education is intended or should be inferred.

Contents

Page

THE NATURE OF MAGNETISM   6

What are magnets and magnetism?   6

How did magnetism get its name?   7

What are magnetic poles?   9

What is the Law of Magnetic Poles?   10

How can you cause magnets to float in air?   11

What are magnetic materials?   12

How does a vending machine reject slugs?   12

How can you make a magnetic slug rejector?   13

What are lines of magnetic force?   14

What is a magnetic field?   15

Can magnetism pass through materials?   16

What is a non-magnetic watch?   18

What is the smallest magnet?   18

How can you make a magnet?   19

What is a permanent magnet?   20

How can you demagnetize a magnet?   22

How can you make a magnetic boat?   22

THE EARTH AS A MAGNET   23

What is geomagnetism?   23

What is the difference between geomagnetism and gravity?   24

Why is a magnet's north pole really a south pole?   24

What is a compass?   25

How do you use a compass?   25

How does a mariner use his compass to guide his ship?   26

What is magnetic declination?   26

How do we know that the earth's magnetic poles wander?   27

Page

How do prospectors use magnetism to find ore?   28

What causes the aurora borealis, or northern lights?   29

What is the Van Allen magnetosphere?   29

ELECTROMAGNETISM   30

How did Oersted discover electromagnetism?   30

How can you perform Oersted's experiment?   31

What is an electromagnet?   32

How can you make an electromagnet?   32

How can a magnet produce electricity?   34

How can you do Faraday's experiment?   34

ELECTROMAGNETS IN USE   34

How does a doorbell work?   34

What is a dynamo?   35

How does an electric motor use magnets?   36

How can you make an electric motor?   38

What part do magnets play in atomic research?   40

MAGNETS IN COMMUNICATION   41

How are magnets used in a telegraph?   41

How does a telephone work?   42

How can you make a telegraph set?   43

How can you make a simple telephone?   45

What part do magnets play in radio and television?   46

YOU AND MAGNETISM   48

MAGNETISM:

In a junk yard, a crane lowers a thick metal disc into a pile of scrap metal. When the disc is raised, the body of an automobile and a few large pieces of iron are attached to it, although no chains or ropes hold these things in place. A refrigerator door is held tightly closed, although it has no latch or lock. Button-sized pieces of metal hold a sheet of paper on a bulletin board with nothing apparently holding them up. In all these instances magnetism is at work.

Your phone rings and then your friend's voice tells you that he is coming to your house. Soon your doorbell rings,

The crane in the junk-yard lifting an automobile, the telephone, the doorbell, the television screen you watch, and the beautiful display of colored lights you may have seen in the northern or southern skies, all have to do, one way or another, with magnetism.

as your friend arrives. Then the two of you watch the images of football players rush back and forth across your television screen. The phone, the doorbell, and the television set could not work if it were not for magnets and magnetism.

You may have seen, in the direction of the polar regions, great glowing curtains of varicolored light sweeping across the night sky. You know these curtains are the northern lights, or *aurora borealis,* or their southern counterpart, the *aurora australis.* This vast display of lights is due to magnetism.

Magnetism plays an increasingly important part in our daily lives as we use more and more household appliances and electrical devices. Scientists probing further and further into the secrets of nature find magnetism to be important everywhere, whether it be within the extremely small nucleus of an atom or in the vast distances of the astronomical universe. Let us investigate this phenomenon we call magnetism by reading about it on the following pages and by performing experiments that help us to understand what we read.

A legend tells us that the word "magnetism" comes from Magnes, a Greek shepherd, whose staff clung to a "magnetic stone."

The Nature of Magnetism

A *magnet* is a piece of metal that has certain unique properties. A magnet can pull toward itself, and hold, pieces of iron. For instance, a small hand-held magnet can pull and hold nails, screws, paper clips, and other things made of iron or steel, which is a kind of iron. A magnet can pull another magnet toward itself or push the other magnet away. What is so remarkable about a magnet is that it can perform its work without actually touching the objects that it pulls or pushes.

What are magnets and magnetism?

We say objects that act like magnets are *magnetized*. The invisible something that enables magnets to pull or push other objects is called *magnetism*. Magnetism cannot be seen, heard, smelled, tasted, or directly felt, and it does not have any weight. Because magnetism cannot be detected by our senses, the only way we can learn anything about it is by noting what it does.

The two kinds of magnets that we will work with are *bar magnets,* which are short straight pieces of metal, and *horseshoe magnets* which are bar mag-

BAR MAGNET

HORSESHOE MAGNET

nets bent into the shape of a horseshoe or the letter U. You can buy magnets in toy stores, hobby shops, and hardware stores.

There is a legend that in ancient Greece a shepherd boy named Magnes, while tending his sheep on Mount Ida, placed his staff on a large stone and found that the stone clung to the tip of the staff so strongly that Magnes could not pull the stone free. The legend goes on to say that from Magnes' name we get the name "magnet," because of a magnetic stone that clung to Magnes' staff. The following explanation is probably closer to the truth. The word "magnet" comes from the name of the city of Magnesia in Asia Minor, near which magnetic stones, or, more accurately, pieces of magnetic iron ore, were found in abundance. The modern name for magnetic iron ore is *magnetite*.

How did magnetism get its name?

The Greeks and Romans knew that a piece of magnetite would attract small pieces of iron even through a bronze or wooden bowl, or when under water. Many strange beliefs grew up about a substance as curious as magnetite. The ancients believed that charms and finger rings made of magnetic stones could attract one's beloved, and that a piece of magnetite placed on your head would make you able to hear the voices of the gods. Magnetic stones also were believed to cure rheumatism, cramps, or gout. Powdered magnetite mixed with oil or grease was said to prevent or cure baldness.

During the Middle Ages, pieces of magnetic iron ore were called *loadstones,* or *lodestones.* They continued to be regarded as amulets and interesting curiosities until someone observed that when a loadstone is suspended by a thread, one end of the loadstone always points north.

Mariners soon made use of this fact. They understood that if one end of a suspended loadstone always points north, then a ship with such a loadstone aboard can always be guided in the direction desired, even when the sun, moon, and stars are hidden by clouds. Loadstone got its name from being used for direction-finding. "Load" was an old English word for "way," and a loadstone was a "way-finding stone."

The ancients attributed to magnets many supernatural qualities that could be used for curing a large number of ills.

One day, somebody discovered that one end of a loadstone, suspended by a thread, always points north.

N

Mariners of the past were afraid of the "mountain of loadstone" which, as the legend goes, could wreck even the most seaworthy vessels.

At left, a primitive compass, consisting of a magnetized needle on a cork floating in water. Columbus used such a compass.

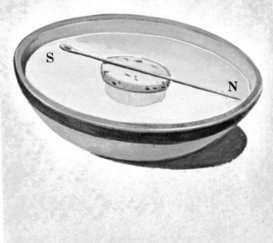

The suspended loadstone was the first compass. Actually, a piece of loadstone hung by a thread did not make a completely satisfactory compass. It was not long before mariners devised a more sensitive compass by magnetizing a large needle (by stroking it on a loadstone) and then thrusting the needle through a piece of reed or cork so that it would float when placed in a bowl filled with water. One end of the needle always pointed north, and this was the first real compass needle.

Even before loadstone was used to guide ships, mariners had a legend about it. They believed that there was a great Mountain of Loadstone. No one knew just where this mountain was located, but it was feared by all mariners who sailed the seas of the Far East. The mariners believed that if a ship sailed too close, the Mountain of Loadstone would attract every piece of iron on board the ship. This would draw the ship irresistibly toward the mountain. As the ship drew closer, all loose pieces of iron would fly straight out to the mountain. Finally, when the ship was very close, the mountain would pull the bolts and nails out of the ship's timbers, and the ship would fall apart. Sinbad the Sailor, one of the heroes in *The Arabian Nights*, was shipwrecked by the Mountain of Loadstone.

What are magnetic poles? If you suspend a bar magnet horizontally by a loop of thread, as shown in the illustration, you will find that when the magnet stops swinging, one end will point north. This end is the *north-seeking pole*, or simply *north pole*, of the magnet. The other end of the magnet is the *south-seeking*, or *south pole*. The north pole may be

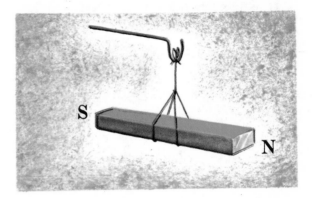

called simply the "N pole," and the south pole the "S pole." No matter in what direction the ends of the magnet may point when you suspend it, and no matter how many times you may perform this experiment, one end will always point north. Later, we will learn why this is so.

Perhaps the first account of the use of the magnet for finding direction comes from China at the time of Hoang-ti, who reigned over his empire nearly 5000 years ago. Pursuing a rebellious prince, he became lost in a dense fog. He found both his way and the enemy by guiding a wonderful chariot he had constructed. Mounted on the front of this chariot was the figure of a woman that could swivel in all directions and that always pointed with one outstretched arm to the south, regardless of the direction in which the chariot was driven. If the legend is true, there must have been a magnet in the figure. (While the western world considers the needle of the compass to point north, the Chinese consider the compass needle as pointing south.)

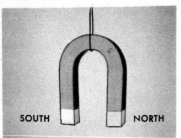

One side of a suspended horseshoe magnet will always point to the north.

If you suspend a horseshoe magnet by a loop of thread around the middle of the horseshoe curve, you will find that when the magnet stops swinging, one side of the horseshoe will always point north. Since we learned that a horseshoe magnet is a bar magnet bent into the shape of a horseshoe, you can easily understand that the north pole of the horseshoe magnet is at the end of the side that points north.

Now is a good time to mark the north and south poles of your magnets. Suspend each magnet by a thread. As soon as you know which is the north pole, mark it on the magnet with an N; mark the other pole with an S. Use pencil, ink, or crayon — whichever will write on your magnet.

What is the Law of Magnetic Poles?

Suspend a magnet as you did when marking its poles. Note which end of the suspended magnet is its N pole. Take another magnet in hand, and, beginning at a distance of ten inches, slowly approach the N pole of the suspended mag-net with the S pole of the magnet in your hand. Soon, you will see the end of the suspended magnet move toward the end of the approaching magnet. If you turn the magnet in your hand around so that its N pole approaches the N pole of the suspended magnet, you will see the suspended magnet swing away from the approaching magnet.

Repeat what you have just done, first, approaching the S pole of the suspended magnet with the N pole of the magnet in your hand. Then approach the S pole of the suspended magnet with the S pole of the magnet in your hand. Note whether the suspended magnet swings toward or away from the approaching magnet each time.

On a sheet of paper print the following table and record by means of check marks in the proper column just how the magnets acted in the experiment you just performed. If necessary, repeat the experiment. Your check marks should appear in the same places as those in the table printed on the bottom of page 11.

What do the locations of the check marks show? They show that *unlike magnetic poles* (a north pole and a south pole) *attract one another, and like magnetic poles* (two north poles or two south poles) *repel one another.* This is the Law of Magnetic Poles.

Experiments to demonstrate the Law of Magnetic Poles.

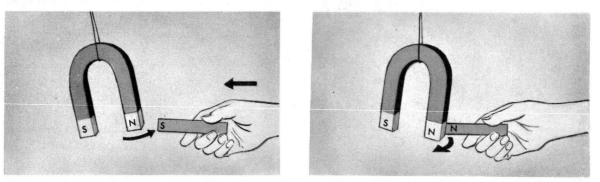

To perform this experiment you will need two power-

How can you cause magnets to float in air?

ful magnets of the kind known as alnico magnets. (Alnico magnets are made of a special kind of metal. You will read more about alnico magnets in another part of this book.)

If you are going to use bar magnets, you will have to make a guide frame in the following manner. Obtain six small sticks about five inches long, such as ice-cream or lollipop sticks. You can also use six pencils. Place a bar magnet on the center of the top of a small cardboard box. Make two pencil marks evenly spaced on either side of the magnet, and two marks a sixteenth of an inch out from each end of the magnet. Now push a stick through both the top and bottom of the box at each pencil mark. Finally, place the second magnet into the frame of sticks surrounding the first magnet. Be sure the north pole of the upper magnet is above the north pole of the lower magnet; then, of course, south pole will be above south pole. The upper magnet will remain suspended in the air, as if by magic. But you know that the reason why the upper magnet hangs unsupported. Like magnetic poles are repelling each other, as we learned they do when we learned the Law of Magnetic Poles.

If you use horseshoe magnets, you will have to make your guide frame as shown in the second illustration on this page.

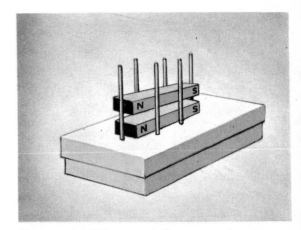

Magnets that "float on air."

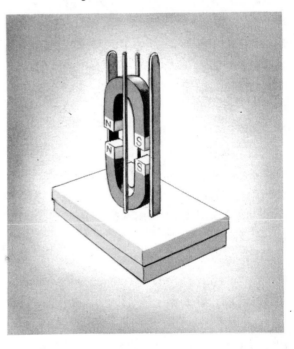

Pole of suspended magnet	Pole of approaching magnet	Poles swing toward (*attract*) one another	Poles swing away from (*repel*) one another
N	S	✓	
N	N		✓
S	N	✓	
S	S		✓

Go around your house trying to pick up

What are magnetic materials? different small objects with your magnets. Try to pick up paper clips, pencils, erasers, rubber bands. See whether your magnets will pick up pieces of paper, wood, plastic, cloth. Try to pick up pebbles, grains of sand, salt, and sugar. See whether you can pick up a nickel, a dime, a quarter.

All the objects that your magnets pick up are made of *magnetic materials*. A magnetic material is one that can be attracted by a magnet. The main magnetic materials are the metals, iron, nickel, and cobalt. Of these three, iron is by far the most magnetic. But there are also mixtures of metals, called alloys, that make materials far more magnetic than iron. Alnico is the name of an alloy made of aluminum, nickel, iron, cobalt, and copper. We learned that we needed very strong or alnico magnets in order to make a magnet float in air.

The more magnetic a material is, the stronger the magnet that can be made of it. Also, the more strongly magnetic a material is, the more easily it is attracted by a magnet. Probably the most magnetic material of all is an alloy that is four-fifths platinum and one-fifth cobalt.

Although there are other magnetic materials, the objects your magnets picked up around your house were probably made of iron or steel. As we have learned, steel is a kind of iron. Materials that are not magnetic are said to be *non-magnetic.*

You probably know that dishonest per-

How does a vending machine reject slugs? sons may try to buy candy, peanuts, ice cream, soda, or other things from vending machines by putting slugs into the coin slot. A slug is a metal washer or other flat circular piece of metal the size of a coin and usually made of iron or steel. To prevent this kind of stealing, the manufacturers build devices into their vending machines that cause the machine to reject slugs. If a slug is put into one of these vending machines, it simply falls through the machine to the coin-return slot, and no merchandise can be obtained from the machine.

Slug rejectors work in different ways. Some vending machines have more than one kind of slug rejector. The following is a description of three kinds of slug-rejectors — two non-magnetic and one magnetic — that may be built into a vending machine. When a coin or slug is put into the coin slot, it rolls down a narrow channel. This channel has a hole just a little smaller than the size of the required coin. A coin rolls over this hole, but a slug smaller than the coin falls through the hole and goes to the coin-return slot. Farther down the channel is a spring attached to a piece of metal blocking the way. The spring cannot be moved by a slug that is lighter than the required coin. A light slug bounces off the piece of metal and falls to the coin-return slot. A slug that goes past the first two slug-rejectors comes to a magnetic slug rejector. Here, the coin or slug, continuing to fall down the narrow channel comes to a branch in the shape of an upside-down V, like this ∧. There is a magnet at the top of one of the branches. When a steel slug falls to the top of the branch in the channel, the slug is pulled down the branch that contains the magnet. The magnet is just strong enough to pull the slug, but not to hold it, so the slug continues down the branch into which it was pulled and then on to the coin-return slot. Coins roll down the other branch of the inverted V, where they release the merchandise.

When you were going around your house testing objects to learn which were made of magnetic materials, you found that coins were non-magnetic. You can see that in a magnetic slug-rejector a coin will not be pulled into the channel that has the magnet.

To make a magnetic slug rejector, you

How can you make a magnetic slug rejector?

will need a strong magnet, a piece of stiff cardboard about the size of a page of this book, some nickels, dimes, or pennies, and a supply of three-quarter-inch steel washers. You can buy the washers at a hardware store.

Draw a line down the middle of both sides of the piece of cardboard. Use adhesive cellophane tape to attach a magnet half an inch from the middle line and halfway from top to bottom of the piece of cardboard. Use some books to prop the cardboard at an angle, as shown in the illustration, with the magnet on the underside.

One by one, place the coins and the slugs at the center of the top of the cardboard, and let them slide down. Just what happens now will depend on how strong your magnet is. If it is weak, it will push the steel washers sidewise a

HOW TO MAKE A SLUG REJECTOR.

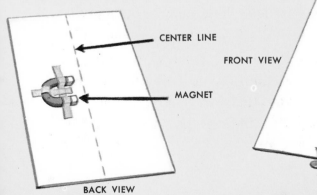

CENTER LINE

MAGNET

FRONT VIEW

BACK VIEW

FRONT VIEW

COINS

WASHERS

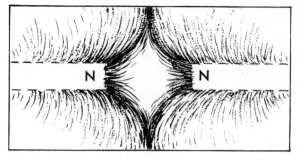

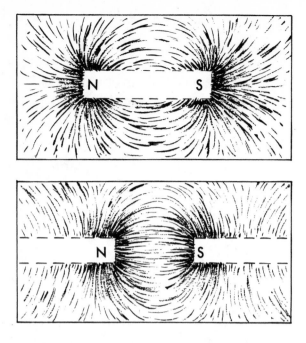

Patterns of lines of magnetic force created by (top left) one bar magnet, (left) two bar magnets with unlike poles opposite each other, (above) two bar magnets with like poles opposite each other.

little bit as they slide past. If the magnet is of medium strength, it will push the washers farther out of the straight-line path down the cardboard. If your magnet is strong, it will hold the steel washers as they reach it in their slide down the cardboard. No matter what the strength of the magnet, the coins will slide past it. Thus, your magnetic slug rejector has separated the slugs from the coins by either pushing the coins sideways, as though into a coin-return channel, or by keeping the slugs from following the coins.

You may wonder why a magnetic slug rejector does not reject nickels, because these coins must certainly be made of nickel, a metal which we learned is magnetic. The answer is that the metal of which a nickel is made is a mixture that is three-fourths copper and one-fourth nickel, and the resulting alloy is only very slightly magnetic.

What are lines of magnetic force?

You have learned that you become aware of magnetism by noting what it does. Now, give magnetism something to do;

make it write its signature. You need a magnet, a sheet of stiff paper (thin cardboard or a thin plate of glass can be used), and about a teaspoonful of iron filings or any other form of iron dust.

If you know someone who works in a machine shop, he will probably give you all the filings you need. Perhaps you know someone who has a grinding wheel and can provide iron particles with little trouble by grinding them from a piece of iron. If you must make your own iron filings, you will find it easy, although a little tiresome. Obtain a large iron nail or any other piece of iron. A carpenter will probably be glad to give you one or two large nails. If possible, clamp the nail firmly in a machinist's vise. If you do not have the use of a vise, hold one end of the nail firmly on a hard surface (not a polished table top!). Place a large sheet of paper beneath the nail to catch the filings. To file the nail, use a medium-coarse machinist's file. Ask a hardware dealer about this kind of file. Be sure not to use a wood file. Now, simply file and file and file, until you have enough iron filings. If you have a hacksaw, you will find that cutting the nail into several pieces is another way to provide yourself with sufficient iron powder from the iron sawdust.

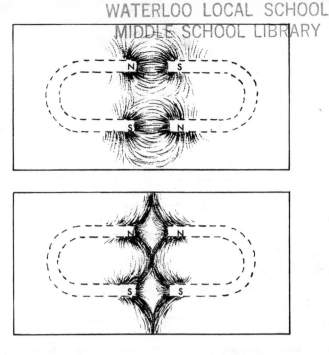

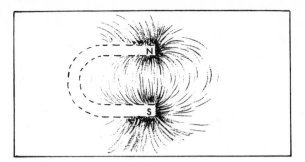

Lines of magnetic force created by, (above) one horseshoe magnet, (top right) two horseshoe magnets unlike poles opposite each other, (right) two horseshoe magnets with like poles opposite each other.

Put a magnet on a table and place your sheet of stiff paper so that it rests upon the magnet. Sprinkle the iron particles slowly and evenly upon the paper, covering the area just above, and for two or three inches on all sides of the magnet. Then, tap the paper lightly several times with a pencil point in order to make certain that the iron particles are spread evenly.

If you have used a bar magnet, the iron particles will arrange themselves in the pattern shown in illustration A on page 14. If you have used a horseshoe magnet, the arrangement of iron particles will be that shown in illustration A at the top of page 15. Lines of iron particles radiate outward from both poles of the magnet. Scientists say that the particles are arranged along *lines of magnetic force*. No one knows exactly what lines of magnetic force are, but they are always present near a magnet. They are invisible, but by making them reveal themselves in a pattern by means of iron particles, you cause the lines of magnetic force to write their signature.

Try the same experiment again, this time placing the north and south poles of two magnets half an inch to an inch apart. Now the lines of magnetic force arrange the iron particles as shown in illustration B on page 14, if you have used bar magnets, and as shown in illustration B on page 15, if you have used horseshoe magnets.

Repeat the experiment once more, this time placing like poles near each other. The particles will be lined up as shown in illustration C on page 14, if you have used bar magnets, and as in illustration C on page 15, if you have used horseshoe magnets.

Note that in all three experiments, the iron particles are thickest at the poles of a magnet. Careful measurements have shown that each pole occupies about one-twelfth the length of a magnet.

Why do we say that the iron filings in the experiment you just performed are arranged by lines of magnetic force? Because when any object is moved or kept from falling, or when an elastic object is bent, stretched, or compressed, we say that a force is acting. You know that a magnet can move magnetic materials without touching them, and it can keep them from falling. You have seen a paper clip jump

What is a magnetic field?

This experiment proves that magnetism passes through non-magnetic materials, while magnetic materials gather the lines of magnetic force and very little magnetism, if any, passes beyond.

up to the pole of a magnet and remain there although nothing you can see is holding the paper clip from falling. A magnet can cause a steel spring — an elastic object — to bend, stretch, or be compressed. Since magnetism can do all the things that show a force is acting, magnetism must be one kind of force. The area in which lines of magnetic force act is called a *magnetic field*.

To do this experiment, you must use an alnico magnet, because other magnets probably will not be strong enough. If you use a bar magnet, build a pile of books about ten inches high. Place the magnet on the books, so that one pole of the magnet projects over the edge of the pile.

Can magnetism pass through materials?

If you use a horseshoe magnet, build two piles of books, each about 15 inches high and ten inches apart. Place a one-foot ruler or a stick the same length across the space between the books. Tie the magnet to the middle of the ruler with a short piece of string, so that the poles hang downward.

Tie a 15-inch piece of string to a paper clip. Push a thumbtack part way into a piece of wood. Wind the thread twice around the thumbtack about five inches from the loose end of the thread. With one hand, hold the paper clip ¼ of an inch away from the magnet. With the other hand, gently pull the loose end of the thread until it is tight. Then push the thumbtack all the way into the wood, securing the thread tightly to the wood. Let go of the paper clip. It will remain suspended in the air, pointing at the magnet.

Carefully, without touching the paper clip, pass between the magnet and the paper clip the following materials: a piece of paper, a piece of cardboard, the corner of an aluminum cookie tin, a piece of plastic sandwich wrapping, a thin flat piece of glass, a silver coin, a penny, a wide rubber band. If you did all this carefully, the paper clip remained suspended in the air while the magnet continued to attract it. This means that magnetism had to pass through each of the materials you placed between the magnet and paper clip. In this experiment you have learned that magnetism can pass through several different kinds of materials. What do all these materials have in common? They all are non-magnetic materials.

Now, pass a penknife blade between the paper clip and the magnet. The paper clip falls down. Put the paper clip back into its suspended position.

Cut one end out of a tin can with a can opener. Slip this piece of metal between the paper clip and the magnet. Again, the paper clip falls. Try this once again, using a large nail in place of the knife blade. When the nail is between the paper clip and the magnet, the paper clip will fall. Why does the paper clip fall when the knife blade, the end of the tin can, and the nail are placed between it and the magnet? The answer must be that magnetism cannot pass through these things. What do they have in common? All of them are made of iron or steel, magnetic materials. (A tin can is made of steel thinly coated with tin.) Magnetism easily passes into a magnetic material, which gathers together the lines of magnetic force, so that little, if any, magnetism passes beyond. Suppose that water is magnetism and a stretched-out handkerchief is a sheet of non-magnetic material. If you pour some water on the handkerchief, the water will flow right through, just as magnetism passes through a non-magnetic material. Now, suppose that a large sponge is a magnetic material. If you pour some water on the sponge, the water will be absorbed into the sponge and none will pass through, just as magnetism is absorbed and does not pass through a magnetic material.

Let us prove in another way what we have just learned. Cut two strips of cardboard two inches wide and about a foot long. Make two piles of books three inches apart. Place the two cardboard strips, one on top of the other, and put both on top of the books. Place more books on each pile. Put a magnet on top of the cardboard strips. Place some tacks (or paper clips) against the bottom of the cardboard, just under the magnet. The tacks will be held up by the magnet.

Slip a knife blade between the two strips of cardboard, just below the magnet. The tacks will fall. Try this experiment again, using the end of the tin can.

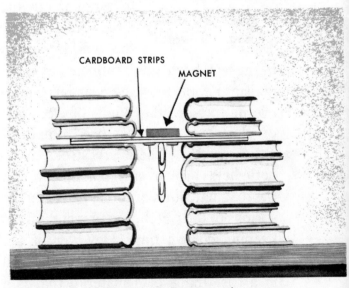

Another experiment to show that magnetism passes through non-magnetic materials.

Again, the tacks fall, as the steel absorbs the magnetic force.

Perhaps, when you bought your horseshoe magnet it had a piece of metal across its poles. If you bought a pair of bar magnets, perhaps they had a piece of metal bridging the two bars at each end. These pieces of metal are called *armatures*, or *keepers*. They are made of a very magnetic metal and ab-

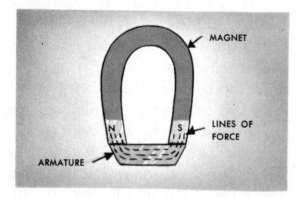

Armatures absorb lines of magnetic force and by doing so preserve the magnet's strength.

sorb the lines of magnetic force. This helps to preserve the strength of the magnet.

You may have seen a watch advertised

What is a non-magnetic watch?

to be non-magnetic. This means that the working parts of the watch will not be affected by magnetism. People working near large electric motors or other kinds of electrical or electronic machines need non-magnetic watches. There are strong magnetic fields around such machinery, and the magnetic lines of force, affecting the springs of the watch, can prevent it from keeping correct time. However, if the working parts of the watch are enclosed in a case made of a material that is a very good magnetic absorber, magnetic

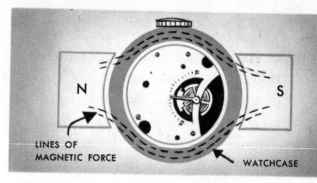

The lines of magnetic force will not reach the spring; they are absorbed by the watch case.

lines of force will be absorbed and held by the watchcase and will not reach the springs of the watch. But this way of making a watch non-magnetic is awkward because a large, thick watch-case is needed.

A new and better way of making a non-magnetic watch has recently been made possible. A non-magnetic steel alloy has been found that can be used to make watch springs. Thus, all the parts of the watch can be made of non-magnetic metals. Magnetism passes entirely through such watches and cannot affect their timekeeping at all.

If you were to break a bar magnet in

What is the smallest magnet?

halves, wouldn't you expect to have one half with a north pole and the other half with a south pole? Yet, if you were to test the

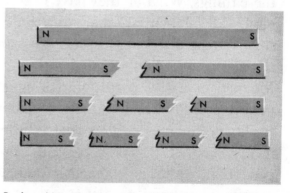

By breaking a magnet in parts, you get little magnets, each one having its own north and south pole.

two halves, you would find that you have two complete magnets, both with north and south poles. If you broke the halves into quarters, and the quarters into eighths, and so on, until you had very small pieces, you would find that each piece is a complete magnet with both a north and a south pole. This fact led the German scientist, Wilhelm Weber, to surmise, a century ago, that each atom of a piece of magnetic material is a magnet, with a north and a south pole of its own. You probably know that all forms of matter are made up of extremely small particles called atoms. Each atom is made up of a central nucleus around which revolve electrically-charged particles called electrons.

Weber's guess was a brilliant one; modern physicists have learned that, as an electron revolves around the nucleus, it spins on its axis and, because of this spin, generates a magnetic field. Thus, an electron is the smallest known magnet.

The magnetic properties of materials are due to the way the atoms of these materials have their electrons' magnetic fields lined up. Magnetic materials have groups of atoms whose magnetic fields are more or less permanently lined up.

These groups of atoms are called *magnetic domains*. In an unmagnetized piece of magnetic material, the domains are arranged in a haphazard manner. As a magnetic material becomes more and more magnetized, more and more of its magnetic domains line up, with their north poles all pointing in one direction and their south poles in the opposite direction. When the majority of its domains have been lined up, a material is magnetized.

Now that we know what causes a material to be magnetic, let us see whether we can find ways to make a magnet. We have to find ways to line up the atoms in the majority of the magnetic domains.

How can you make a magnet?

Pick up a paper clip with a magnet. Touch another paper clip to the end of the one the magnet is holding. The second paper clip is held to the first. See how many paper clips your magnet will hold in a chain. Each paper clip in the chain must act as a magnet in order to hold the one below it. This means that simply by touching the paper clip to a pole of the magnet, the magnetic domains in the paper clip are lined up, and

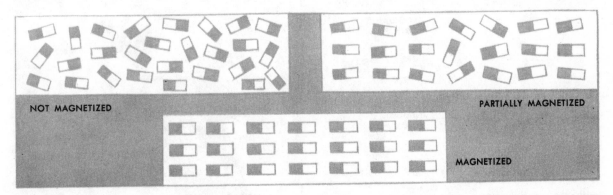

The illustration shows schematically how atoms are arranged in an unmagnetized bar magnet, in one that is partially magnetized, and in one that is completely magnetized.

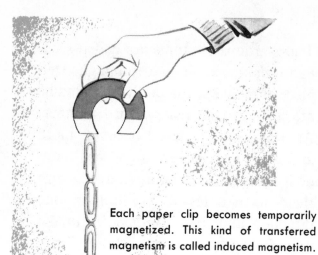

Each paper clip becomes temporarily magnetized. This kind of transferred magnetism is called induced magnetism.

the largest magnet we have — the earth itself. Striking the bar helped to disturb the atoms in their magnetic domains, so that the magnetic field of the earth could line them up with their north poles pointing in one direction and their south poles in the other.

the paper clip becomes magnetized. Magnetism transferred in this way from magnetized material to unmagnetized material is called *induced magnetism*.

If you can obtain a steel bar about two feet long and half an inch in diameter, you can magnetize the bar in a simple way. Hold the bar so that it points in the direction that a compass needle points. Holding the bar in this position, strike the end of it hard 20 times with a hammer. Now, see whether the ends of the bar will pick up iron filings or paper clips. They will, and you have made a magnet. Pointing the bar north lined it up parallel to the field of

What is a permanent magnet?

Make a chain of paper clips, as you did when learning about induced magnetism. Pull the uppermost paper clip away from the magnet. The chain falls apart. Try to pick up one paper clip with another; it cannot be done, because none of the paper clips are magnetized any longer.

Let us try harder to make a paper clip into a magnet. Stroke the paper clip across one pole of a magnet. Do not stroke the paper clip back and forth; stroke it in one direction only, lifting it off the magnet when you come to one end and putting the other end back on the magnet. When you have completed 20 strokes, see whether the paper clip will pick up other paper clips. It will not. This means that it cannot retain the

Striking the steel bar with a hammer helps to disturb the atoms in their magnetic domains enough to line them up with the earth's magnetic field.

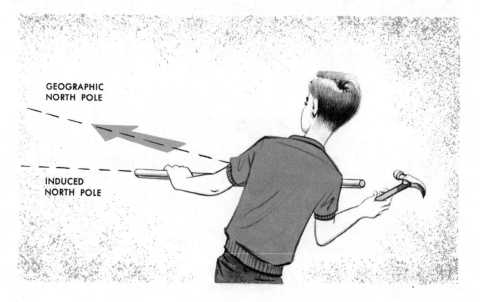

GEOGRAPHIC NORTH POLE

INDUCED NORTH POLE

magnetism induced in it by the magnet. In both these experiments, you may find that a small amount of magnetism *does* remain in the paper clips. This little bit of left-over magnetism is called *residual magnetism*. It will gradually disappear with the passing of time.

Clearly, the magnetism induced in the paper clips is temporary. Magnets that lose all, or almost all, of their magnetism when they are no longer in a magnetic field are called *temporary magnets*. The atoms of the magnetic domains of materials that make temporary magnets are easily lined up, even by weak magnetic fields, but they just as easily lose their alignment when removed from the magnetic field.

Obtain a large sewing needle. Stroke the needle several times across one pole of a magnet. Stroke the needle just as you did the paper clip, not back and forth, but in one direction only, lifting it off the magnet when you come to one end, and putting the other end back on the magnet. When you have done this about 20 times, place the magnet out of reach and see whether the needle will pick up a small paper clip or some iron filings. It will. Since the needle is no longer in the magnet's field and yet remains magnetized, you can see that the atoms of the needle's magnetic domains must remain lined up after they are removed from the magnetic field. If you put the needle away and test it again tomorrow or a week or a month from now, you will find that it is still magnetized. Magnets made from materials that remain magnetized after being removed from a magnetic field are called *permanent magnets*.

A remarkable thing about inducing temporary or permanent magnets is that, no matter how many new magnets are made, the original magnet does not lose any of its magnetism. You could magnetize millions of needles from a small magnet and the magnet would remain as strong as when you began.

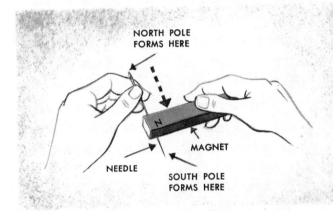

To make a permanent magnet out of a sewing needle, you have to stroke the needle in one direction only with one pole of a magnet.

Permanent magnets have many uses. Placed in a roller at the end of a conveyor belt carrying iron ore and pieces of rock, a permanent magnet holds the iron ore on the belt as it turns over the roller. As a result, the iron ore falls in one pile and the unwanted rock shoots off into another pile. In the same way, stray pieces of iron are separated from coal; but this time, it is the iron that is unwanted. Permanent magnets pick stray pieces of iron out of flour, chemicals, and textiles. A large permanent magnet lowered on the end of a rope is used by police to drag rivers or lakes for guns or other steel objects. A small permanent magnet lowered on the end of a string may be used to retrieve small iron or steel objects dropped into the drain-pipes of sinks.

If you have the steel bar you magnetized

How can you demagnetize a magnet? by striking its end, hold it so that it runs along an east-west line. Strike the bar several times, on its sides as well as its end. Now test it to see whether it still is magnetic. It is not. By jarring the atoms of the magnetic domains in the bar, you cause them to lose their alignment, so that their north and south poles cancel each other out, and the bar is no longer magnetized.

Another way to demagnetize a magnet is to heat it. With a pair of pliers, grasp the needle you magnetized and hold it in a flame until it is red hot. Place it in an east-west direction and let it cool. Then try to pick up a paper clip with the needle. You will find that the needle has lost its magnetism. The heat caused the atoms of the needle to move about very rapidly and, in doing so, to disarrange themselves.

A heated magnet loses its magnetism at a very definite temperature. This temperature is called the *Curie point,* for its discoverer, Pierre Curie, a French scientist. Each magnetic material has its own Curie point. For iron it is about 800° Centigrade; for nickel, about 350° Centigrade.

When we say that a demagnetized material has lost its magnetism, we do not mean that the magnetism has gone out of the material or that the magne-

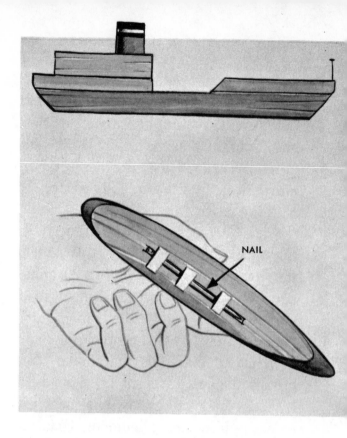

tism has been destroyed. Each atom and each electron is just as much a magnet as when the material was magnetized, but the tiny magnets are no longer lined up so as to produce one big magnet.

Now that you know jarring and heating will result in demagnetizing, you should avoid dropping, pounding, or heating your magnets.

Use a toy boat, or whittle one out of a piece of wood.

How can you make a magnetic boat? Cut the head off an iron nail or use a headless nail, the kind called a "finishing nail." If you are using a wooden boat, cut a short slot in its bottom. The slot should be just big enough for the nail to fit into it. If the nail fits the slot snugly, you will not have to do anything more to keep it in place. If the nail does not fit tightly into the slot, or if you are using a boat into which you cannot cut a slot, attach the nail to the bottom of the boat with waterproof

Heat can demagnetize a magnet.

THE BOAT WITH THE "MAGNETIC MOTOR"

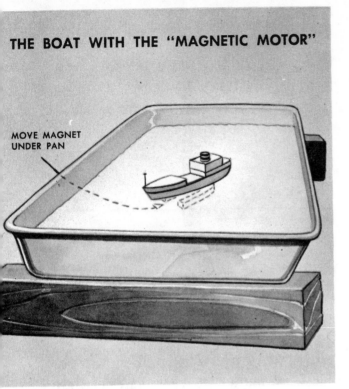

MOVE MAGNET UNDER PAN

cement or with strips of adhesive tape such as doctors use when bandaging.

Using bricks or blocks of wood, prop up an aluminum pan or a wooden or china bowl so that you can move your hand around beneath it. The pan or bowl should be large enough, when filled with water, to float your boat in it. When you have floated the boat, move a magnet around on the underside of the pan. You will be able to make the boat sail wherever you wish.

Instead of a boat, you might use a toy fish or whittle one out of wood. Your magnetic fish will swim wherever you make it go with your magnet.

The Earth as a Magnet

The earth itself is a huge magnet, and

What is geomagnetism?

it creates lines of force (a magnetic field) around it as if a powerful bar magnet were thrust through its diameter from north to south. Most geophysicists — the scientists who specialize in the study of such effects — believe that the earth's magnetism is caused by certain movements in its inner and outer cores. The cores are presumed to be made of a combination of nickel and iron, are under tremendous pressure, and are very hot. The inner core is calculated to be a sphere (probably solid) 1,600 miles in diameter. An outer core, 1,400 miles thick and 1,800 miles beneath the earth's surface, surrounds the inner one like a somewhat stiff paste. The movements within these cores (termed mag-

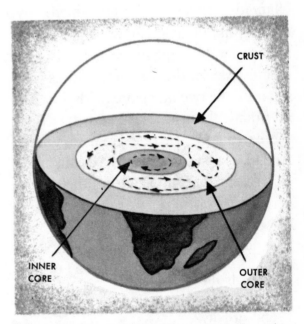

Scientists believe that the main source of the earth's magnetism is within the cores of the earth.

netohydrodynamic motions) act as a natural dynamo and develop electric currents which in turn set up the earth's principal magnetic field.

23

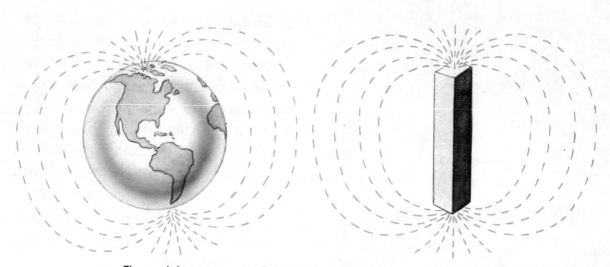

The earth has a magnetic field of force just as a bar magnet does.

A second, much weaker magnetic field is produced by the earth's ionosphere (eye-ON-oh-sfeer), the section of atmosphere directly above the stratosphere which ranges from fifty to three hundred miles out into space. The ionosphere is composed of electrically charged particles (*ions*) which, by moving about in great windlike gusts, also generate a magnetic field. In the strictest sense, then, scientists thus can separate the two magnetic fields, but for all practical purposes we can state that the earth has just one great magnetic field. Because *geo* means "earth," the earth's magnetism is given the name *geomagnetism*.

The earth's magnetic field must not be

What is the difference between geomagnetism and gravity?

confused with its gravity. An unsupported object tends to fall toward the earth's surface. "Falling" means being pulled toward the earth by the force of gravity, and thus seems much like the attraction a magnet has for magnetic materials.

But gravity exerts its pull on *all* objects, no matter of what material they are made. There are no "gravitational poles" on objects to compare with a magnetized object's magnetic poles. The earth's magnetic pull is quite weak, compared to its gravitational pull. For example, an ordinary small steel magnet of the bar or "horseshoe" type has a magnetic field about *ten times* as strong as the earth's magnetic field, while an alnico magnet's field is almost a *hundred times* as strong!

When you learned that the north pole

Why is a magnet's north pole really a south pole?

of a magnet is the north-pointing pole, did you wonder why one pole of a magnet always points north? You know that opposite magnetic poles attract; might it not be that the north pole of a magnet is *attracted* northward? That is exactly what happens. The north-pointing pole of a magnet is attracted northward by a huge magnet — the earth, itself.

Oddly, then, the north-pointing pole

of a magnet must really be a south pole! This is true because unlike magnetic poles attract. So, the south pole of a magnet is attracted northward by the north magnetic pole of the earth. This means that the north pole, or north-pointing pole, of a magnet is really a south pole. However, the north-pointing pole of a magnet is called the north pole, and you must think of it as a north pole when you work with magnets.

A compass needle is simply a thin magnet balanced on a pivot in a manner that permits the magnet to turn easily. As a result, the earth's north magnetic pole attracts one end of the compass needle, so that it always points north. Probably because the earliest use of a magnet as a compass took place in the northern hemisphere, we talk about a compass needle always pointing north. We could just as correctly pay attention to the other pole, the south pole of the magnetic needle, and say that a compass always points south. The more scientific way of describing how a compass needle acts is to say that it points along a north-south line.

What is a compass?

A woodsman's compass, or scouting compass, looks something like a pocket watch. The dial of the compass has the four geographical directions printed on it: north (N), south (S), east (E), and west (W). These four directions are called the *cardinal points* of the compass. Usually, printed between the cardinal points are at least four other compass points: northeast (NE), southeast (SE), southwest (SW), and northwest (NW). The compass needle rests on a pivot raised up from the center of the dial. The dial and needle are contained in a metal case covered by glass to keep out dust.

How do you use a compass?

Suppose you are lost in the woods on a cloudy day. You cannot use the sun

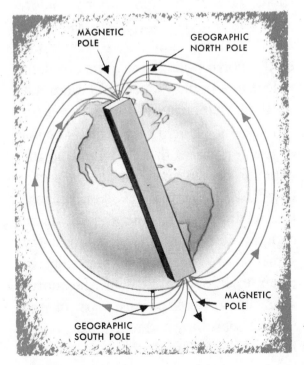

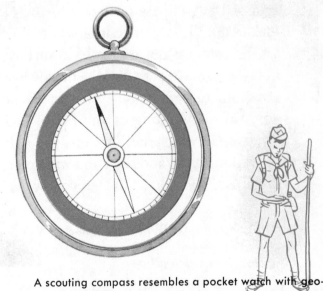

A scouting compass resembles a pocket watch with geographical directions instead of numbers on the dial.

The north-pointing pole of a magnet is really a south pole, and the south-pointing pole a north pole.

to guide you, and you know that if you walk in the direction that you think is home, you will probably walk in circles, as do most people lost in the woods. You must depend on your compass to guide you safely home.

Let's say you know that if you walk due west, you will come to a landmark, perhaps a road or a river or stream, that will lead you home. You place your compass on a flat rock, a tree stump, or some other level surface. When the compass needle stops swinging, you know that it is pointing north. Looking at the dial, you find that the part of the dial beneath the north pole of the needle probably does not read N, or north. To remedy this, you carefully turn the compass, keeping the needle as still as possible, until the N on the compass dial is directly beneath the north-pointing arm of the needle. As a result, the N on the dial faces north, S south, E east, and W west.

You pick up the compass and walk in the direction of the W on the dial, meanwhile keeping the north-pointing arm of the compass needle over the N on the dial. Every once in a while, you set the compass down on a level surface in order to make sure that the needle has not been turned away by tilting when you walked. As long as you follow the direction in which the W points, you will be walking west, and soon you will come to the landmark that will lead you home.

A mariner's compass is one in which

How does a mariner use a compass to guide his ship?

a circular card rests on the magnet. On the card are printed 32 compass points and 360 equal divisions, or degrees. Every apprentice seaman must learn to recite all 32 compass points in correct order, beginning with north and going clockwise around the dial. Doing this is called "boxing the compass." The circular card is attached to the magnet so that the north pole of the magnet is directly beneath the N mark on the card. Thus, when the compass needle points north, the N on the card points north.

At the rim of the mariner's compass there is a mark that is in a straight line with the bow, or front, of the ship. When the helmsman steers the ship so that the N on the dial card points directly to this mark, then the ship is sailing north. If he wants to sail northwest, he turns the ship so that NW on the dial points directly to the mark.

The magnetic pole of the earth's northern hemisphere is

What is magnetic declination?

not located at the North Pole, but at 76° north latitude and 102° west longitude. This is a point approximately 2,000 miles due north of Bismarck, North Dakota, and 1,000 miles south of the north pole. The south magnetic pole is at a point about 2,300 miles due south of Melbourne, Australia.

It was not long after mariners began to use compasses that they realized the compass needle does not point directly north. We know that this is so because the north magnetic pole and the north geographic pole are not located at the same point. Mariners learned that in order to know how to sail due north when they were in any part of the world's seas, they had to know just how far away from geographic north their

N

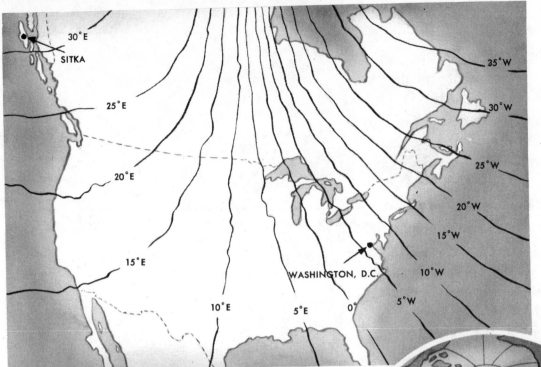

Typical distribution of magnetic declination in the United States.

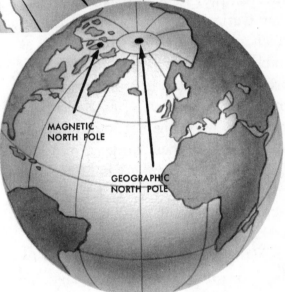

Geographic north and south poles and magnetic north and south poles are not at identical spots.

compass was pointing. They measured the angle between geographic north and magnetic north. They called this difference the *angle of magnetic declination.* For example, at Washington, D. C., the angle of magnetic declination between true north and magnetic north is 6° W, and in Sitka, Alaska, 30° E. This means that at Washington, D. C., geographic north is 6° to the west of where the north pole of a compass points; in Sitka, north is 30° east of north on the compass.

How do we know that the earth's magnetic poles wander?

The earth's magnetic poles are constantly moving about. The movement is slow, but scientists can easily measure it. In 1955, United States government scientists carefully determined the location of the north magnetic pole. Five years later, they repeated the measurements to locate the pole and found that it had moved approximately 70 miles toward the northwest. Throughout millions of centuries, the north and south magnetic poles have actually wandered about the earth. There were times in the past when the north magnetic pole was located in Korea, or the middle of the North Atlantic Ocean, and possibly even Africa. Even more remarkable, the polarity has been reversed — that is, the north and south poles have changed places! It is estimated that 171 such reversals have occurred in the past 80 million years, though no one knows why it happened. The changes do not take place with any apparent regularity. Fixed polarity has ranged, in varying intervals, from thirty thousand years to two million years. How do we know this? The information comes from lava containing grains of the mineral magnetite, or loadstone, that once flowed from prehistoric volcanoes. When the rock is very hot, the grains are not magnetized, since (as we have learned) high temperatures demagnetize magnetic materials. When the lava cools, however, the grains of magnetite reach their Curie point (the temperature at which magnetism is destroyed and at which it reappears, upon cooling) before the lava hardens into rock, at which time the earth's magnetic field lines them up in the north-south direction. The lava then hardens, and the magnetic grains can no longer move around. Millions of years later, when scientists examine the rock formed from the lava, thousands of "compass needles" (the grains of magnetite) point to where the north and south magnetic poles were when the rock was formed.

Many kinds of rock form from sediments carried to oceans and lakes by rivers and streams. In the course of millions of years, the grains of sediment are turned into sedimentary rocks by great pressure within the earth. Some of the grains of the future sedimentary rock are grains of magnetite. As these grains are carried along by the water, they are free to turn along a north-south line under the influence of the earth's magnetic poles. When the grains of sediment have become sedimentary rock, the rock contains tiny "compass

needles." From them, future scientists can tell the location of the earth's magnetic poles when the rocks formed.

The earth's magnetic field is not only stronger at the magnetic poles, but also varies slightly from place to place on the surface of the earth. This is due to the presence in the earth of magnetic materials such as bodies of iron, nickel, or cobalt ore. Prospectors found that if they could measure the changes in the earth's magnetic field, they could tell where to mine for valuable metal ores. At first, making a magnetic survey of an area was very slow, because the instruments that made the measurements had to be carried from place to place, sometimes over very rugged country. But today, a very sensitive measuring instrument, called a *magnetometer,* is placed in a bomb-

How do prospectors use magnetism to find ore?

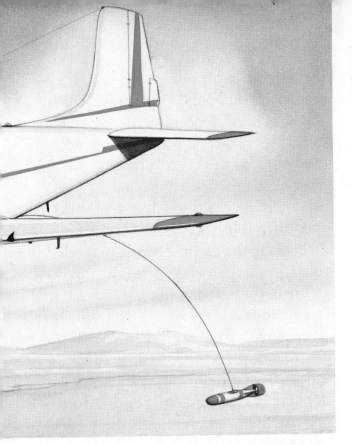

surface of the earth along lines of magnetic force. Many of these particles collide with air molecules causing the molecules to vibrate and give off the white, red, blue, and green lights that make up the awesome displays of the auroras. The auroras are seen only in the higher latitudes because the earth's magnetic field is strongest at the north and south magnetic poles.

What is the Van Allen magnetosphere? Not long after the United States began to put satellites into orbit, scientists found that the earth was surrounded by a huge swarm of highly charged atomic particles extending 50,000 miles out into space. Just where all these hundreds of billions of highly charged particles come from is not known, but large numbers do come from the sun and are trapped by the earth's magnetic field. At first, scientists thought that there were two great belts of radiation surrounding the earth, a small inner belt, a space without radio-

shaped casing and is towed at the end of a long cable beneath an airplane. The sensitive unit in a magnetometer, only the size of a cigarette, has led geophysicists to underground ore 1,500 feet below a plane!

What causes the aurora borealis, or northern lights? If you live in the northern part of the United States or in Canada, or in the southern part of the southern hemisphere, you probably have seen great curtains and streamers of light sweeping through the sky at night, especially during the early spring and fall. These lights are the *aurora borealis*, or northern lights. In the southern hemisphere these lights are called the *aurora australis*, or southern lights.

The sun is continually sending out streams of electrically-charged particles. When these particles reach the earth's magnetic field, they spiral toward the

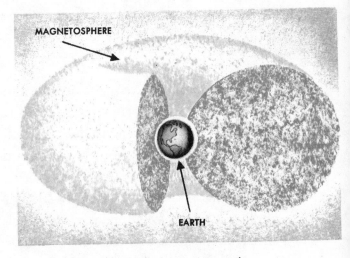

MAGNETOSPHERE

EARTH

The Van Allen radiation magnetosphere.

active particles, and a vast outer belt. Later, scientists learned that their satellites had not covered all the area in which the particles exist. When exploring satellites had covered the whole area, scientists learned that there is only one great swarm of highly charged particles, very dense near the earth and becoming thinner until it ends 50,000 miles out in space. The single swarm was then named the *magnetosphere*. The presence of the charged particles was first discovered by the American physicist, James Van Allen, and the magnetosphere is named for him.

The Van Allen magnetosphere resembles a doughnut that is thickest above the earth's equator where the earth's magnetic field is the weakest. The magnetosphere is quite thin in the northern and southern latitudes near the magnetic poles, where the earth's magnetic field is the strongest. The reason for this is that the electrically-charged particles have magnetic fields. As they arrive from the sun and begin to cross the earth's magnetic field, they are pushed and pulled sideways. Which way they move depends on the direction that their magnetic poles face in relation to the earth's magnetic poles. Since most of the particles are spinning, they are alternately attracted and repelled, and, therefore, they spiral back and forth along the earth's lines of magnetic force. (Some particles move fast enough to break through the lines of magnetic force and reach the earth's atmosphere or even the earth's surface.) The particles that approach the earth parallel to the north and south magnetic poles do not have to cross lines of magnetic force and are pulled straight into the earth's atmosphere by the very powerful attraction of the earth's magnetic poles. This is why the Van Allen magnetosphere is thinnest near the poles.

Space explorers will have to find ways to shield themselves from the radioactive particles of the Van Allen magnetosphere, because these particles can endanger the lives of astronauts.

 # Electromagnetism

For more than 200 years scientists had

How did Oersted discover electromagnetism?

suspected that there was a connection between electricity and magnetism. It was not until 1820 that Hans Christian Oersted, a Danish scientist, proved the connection. One day, Oersted, who was a professor of physics, accidently placed a compass near a wire carrying an electric current. The compass needle had been parallel to the wire. To Oersted's surprise, the compass needle turned away from its north-south line and pointed crosswise to the wire. Oersted tried this several times and found that the compass needle moved only when current was flowing through the wire. He then understood that a wire carrying a current has a magnetic field around it.

To do this experiment and others that follow, it is best to use an electric switch. You can buy an inexpensive one in a hardware store, but it is much more fun to make one.

How can you perform Oersted's experiment?

Using a pair of tin-shears, cut from a tin can a strip of metal about three inches long and half an inch wide. Be careful not to cut yourself on the sharp edges of the tin! Obtain a piece of wood about the size of a small book. Scrape the insulation off the ends of a piece of wire six inches long. Twist one end of the wire around a small nail near its head. Use this nail to attach one end of the tin strip to the piece of wood. Make sure that you hammer the nail all the way down, so that the wire around it presses the tin firmly to the wood. Bend the piece of tin into two angles, as shown in the illustration on page 23.

Make a mark on the wood under, and ¼ of an inch before, the free end of the tin strip. Turn the strip of tin aside. Hammer a nail into the mark you made on the wood until only half an inch of the nail remains out of the wood. Return the tin strip to its original position. When you push down on the end of the strip, it should touch the head of the nail beneath it. Now you have made a switch. (Never use this switch with any source of electricity other than a dry-cell battery. If you do, you will receive a painful shock, or even kill yourself!)

To do Oersted's experiment, you need a compass, a dry-cell battery, and some wire. You can probably buy all three in a five-and-ten-cent store, and certainly in a hardware store. The kind of wire called "bell wire" is best.

Scrape the insulation off both ends of a piece of wire about two feet long. Twist one end of this wire around the nail beneath the end of the tin strip. Attach the other end of wire to the center binding post of the dry cell. Scrape the insulation off both ends of a piece of wire three feet long. Attach one end of this wire to the other binding post of the dry cell, and twist the other end together with the free end of the wire that you nailed to the board.

Place a compass near your switch. Hold a portion of the long wire across the face of the compass. Make sure the north-seeking pole of the compass needle points to the N on the face of the compass and parallel to the wire. Now, push down on your switch to close the electric circuit and make electricity flow from the battery through the wires. What happens to the compass needle? It turns crosswise to the wire. Release the switch. The needle swings back to its normal north-south line. Push and release the switch a few more times. You will see that it is only when electric current is flowing through the wire that the needle swings crosswise to the wire. This proves a current flowing through a wire sets up a magnetic field around the wire (see page 33).

Disconnect the two wires from the binding posts of the battery. Switch them around, that is, connect the long wire to the center binding post and the shorter wire to the other binding post. This change will make the current in the wire flow in the opposite direction. Hold the wire across the compass, as before, and push the switch. This time, the compass needle swings in the opposite direction from that which it did when the wires were connected the other way. This shows that a change in the direction of the current in the wire reverses the direction of the poles of the magnetic field set up around the wire.

We have learned that a current-carrying wire produces a magnetic field around itself. Might

What is an electromagnet?

not this fact be used to make some kind of magnet? Yes, an *electromagnet*. An electromagnet consists of a bar of magnetic material around which are wound many turns of wire. When an electric current is sent through the wire, the lines of magnetic force produced by the current are concentrated in the bar. The bars of electromagnets are usually made of soft iron or any alloy that is easily magnetized and, therefore, easily demagnetized. When the current stops running through the wire, the bar loses practically all its magnetism immediately. In the opening sentence of this book, we read about a large magnet that picked up scrap iron and steel in a junk yard. This kind of magnet is an electromagnet. You can see that if an electromagnet did not lose its magnetism when the current is turned off, the junkyard magnet could not drop the objects that it picks up; they would stick to it until someone pulled them off. Such a magnet would be hard to use.

Obtain a bolt about three inches long and a nut to fit on the bolt. Screw the nut on

How can you make an electromagnet?

the bolt only far enough so that the bottom of the bolt just begins to protrude from the nut. Beginning a foot from the end of a long piece of bell wire, wind the wire around the bolt, starting at the head of the bolt and working toward the nut. Each turn of the wire should touch the one before it. Cover the length of the bolt with two or three layers of wire, making sure that, as you wind back and forth, you continue to wind in the same direction. Leave a foot of wire when you reach the last turn. To secure the wire, slip its end under the last turn. Scrape the insulation off the free ends of the wire, and twist one end around the end of the wire that is secured to the switch you made. Attach the other end to a binding post of your dry cell. Now, attach a wire from the nail of your switch to the other binding post of the dry cell. Hold the end of the bolt over a pile of paper clips and push the switch. The bolt has become an electromagnet that picks up the paper clips. Release the switch. The paper clips drop off the bolt. (It is possible that you may have used a hard steel bolt. If you did, you made a permanent magnet of the bolt, and it will continue to hold the paper clips.) You can make a stronger electromagnet by winding more turns of wire about the bolt, or by connecting the electromagnet to more than one dry cell.

Electric current flowing through a wire sets up a magnetic field.

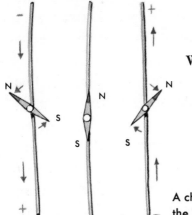

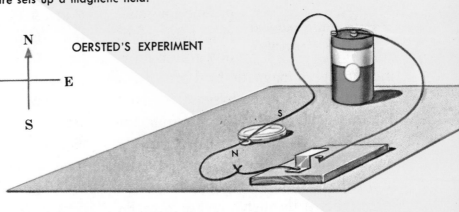

OERSTED'S EXPERIMENT

A change in the direction of the current in the wire reverses the direction of the poles of the magnetic field.

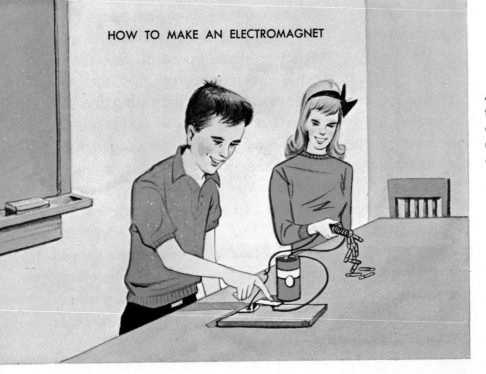

HOW TO MAKE AN ELECTROMAGNET

After having made your electromagnet, you can mount it as shown below to make a miniature electromagnetic crane.

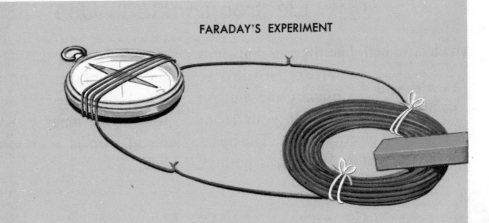

FARADAY'S EXPERIMENT

How to induce electricity by moving a magnet within a coil of wire is described on page 34. When you stop moving the magnet, no electricity will be induced.

If a current flowing through a wire can produce a magnetic field, might not a wire moving through a magnetic field produce a current? The British physicist, Michael Faraday, pondered this question for years and performed many experiments without success. Finally, in 1820, by accident, he found that when he poked a bar magnet through a coil of wire, he produced an electric current in the wire. He then found that it made no difference whether he moved the magnet through the coil of wire or the coil of wire over the magnet. Both actions produced an electric current.

How can a magnet produce electricity?

Wind about 20 turns of bell wire around a paper cup, beginning a foot from the end of the wire. Collapse the cup, leaving a coil of wire. Tie the wires of the coil together with pieces of string at opposite sides of the coil. Wind about four turns of bell wire around a compass so that the wire passes over the face of the compass. Connect the ends of this wire to the ends of the wire from the

How can you do Faraday's experiment?

coil. When a current flows in the wire, a magnetic field will be produced and the compass needle will move. (See page 33 for illustration of the experiment.)

Poke a bar magnet into the coil. The compass needle will move. Note in which direction it moved. Pull the magnet out. The compass needle moves in the opposite direction. This means, of course, that when the magnet reverses its direction, the direction of the current is reversed. Hold the magnet still and move the coil. The results are the same as if you moved the magnet.

Try stopping the movement of the magnet at different parts of the coil. As soon as the motion stops, the compass needle stops moving, indicating that the current has stopped flowing. Therefore, we can guess that it is motion of a wire through a magnetic field that produces an electric current. This guess is right. From this experiment we learn that we need three things to generate electricity in this manner: we need a magnet, a conductor such as wire through which the electric current flows, and motion. If any of these things is lacking, no electricity will be generated.

Electromagnets In Use

An electric bell, like the one that rings when someone pushes the button outside your front door, uses an electromagnet. The push-button is a switch. When it is pushed,

How does a doorbell work?

electric current flows into the coils of the electromagnet on the bell, and a metal strip called the *armature* is pulled toward the magnet. At the top of the metal strip is a knob that strikes the bell.

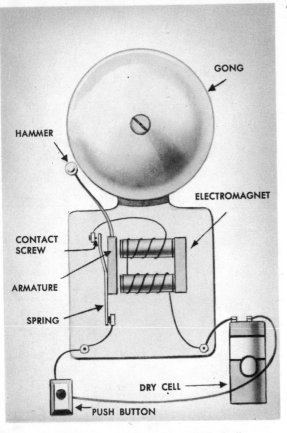

The working parts of an electric bell.

electromagnet no longer pulls on the armature. The brass strip springs back, pulling the armature with it and touching the contact screw again. The circuit is established once more, and the whole sequence of events repeats itself as long as you push on the button.

A buzzer works exactly like a bell, but it makes a buzzing sound instead of a musical sound because in a buzzer, the knob strikes a solid object, instead of a hollow bell.

What is a dynamo? We learned that moving a conductor (the coil of of wire) through a magnetic field produces an electric current. In 1832, the French inventor

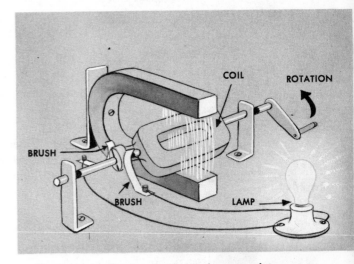

The dynamo changes mechanical energy into electrical energy by electromagnetic induction.

It is reasonable to think that once you push the switch and close the circuit, the armature will be pulled toward the electromagnet and remain there until you release the switch. But you know that this is not what happens when you push the button of a doorbell. Instead, as long as you hold your finger on the button, the armature leaps rapidly back and forth, banging the knob on the bell. How does this happen? The armature is attached to a springy strip of brass that is in contact with a pointed screw, called the *contact screw*. The electric current enters the electromagnet through the contact screw. As soon as the electromagnet pulls the armature, the attached strip of brass also is pulled toward the electromagnet and away from the contact screw, breaking the circuit. When this happens, there is no electric current in the circuit, and the

Hyppolyte Pixii made use of this fact to invent the first device for generating a steady electric current. He made the first electric generator, or *dynamo*. When the coil is turned around within the magnetic field, electric current is generated in the wires that make up the coil. The current flows into the axle and through the contacts to the conductors which are wires. The wires can lead to an electrical appliance, such as a light bulb, an electric iron, a radio, or dozens of other devices that are powered by electricity.

In a modern electric generating plant, such as the one that supplies electricity to your home, there may be one or more huge dynamos having magnets ten feet high and armatures containing tens of thousands of turns of wire. The armatures are turned in the magnetic field by turbines powered by steam or by water falling from a dam.

Below, the working parts of a simple D.C. motor.

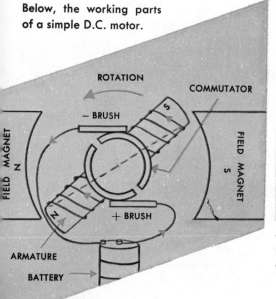

ROTATION

COMMUTATOR

− BRUSH

FIELD MAGNET
N

FIELD MAGNET
S

S

N

+ BRUSH

ARMATURE

BATTERY

Above, closeup of a toy motor connected to two dry cells (batteries).

How does an electric motor use magnets?

We have learned that like magnetic poles repel, and unlike poles attract, each other. This Law of Magnetic Poles is the principle behind an electric motor. An electric motor consists of one magnet turning inside another due to their poles alternately attracting and repelling one another.

Suspend a magnet as you did when learning the Law of Magnetic Poles. Bring the N pole of another magnet near the N pole of the suspended magnet. The N pole of the suspended magnet will, of course, swing away from the approaching N pole of the magnet in your hand. As soon as the N pole of the suspended magnet has made a quarter turn, bring the N pole of the magnet in your hand near the approaching S pole of the suspended magnet. Doing this will attract the swinging S pole. Pull the magnet in your hand out of the way, and as the S pole swings past, turn the magnet in your hand so that its S pole gives the swinging S pole a push. By alternately pushing and pull-

A toy motor you have bought, or one you have constructed yourself, can drive a small fan, just as a big fan is driven by a large electric motor.

When the wire is the coil of an electromagnet, reversing the direction of the current reverses the electromagnet's poles.

The magnet that forms the outer part of an electric motor is stationary. This magnet, called the *field magnet*, may be an electromagnet or a permanent magnet, but its poles do not change. The second magnet, called the *armature*, is located between the poles of the field magnet. The armature, attached to a rod that enables it to spin around, has a coil of wire wound around it. When current enters the wires of the coil, the armature becomes an electromagnet. The like poles of the armature and field magnet repel and the unlike poles attract. As a result the armature turns. When unlike poles come into position near each other, they should stop the armature from turning any farther, if nothing else happens.

Just before the unlike poles face each

ing the poles of the suspended magnet with the magnet in your hand, you can make the suspended magnet revolve quite rapidly. An electric motor works in a similar manner.

At least one magnet in an electric motor must be an electromagnet. This is so because an electromagnet can be made to change its poles when the direction of the electric current is reversed. You remember that Oersted learned that if he changed the direction of the electric current in a wire, it acted like a magnet whose poles are reversed.

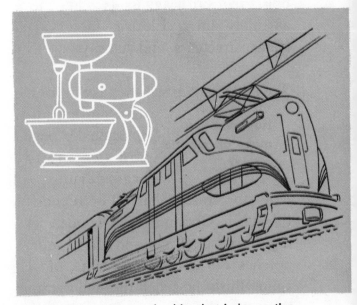

A small kitchen mixer and a big electric locomotive are both driven by electric motors.

37

other, a little device on the armature reverses the direction of the current. This reversing device is called a *commutator*. The reversal of the direction of the current reverses the poles of the armature. Now, the unlike poles that were facing each other are like poles repelling each other. The armature now makes another turn.

As rapidly as the armature spins, the current reverses, and the armature goes on turning as long as current is supplied to the motor. Some armatures turn more than a thousand revolutions a minute.

An electric motor is one of the most useful pieces of machinery we have. We snap a switch, and an electric motor works immediately, powerfully, and quietly. Just think how clumsy it would be to run a kitchen mixer or an air conditioner with a gasoline or steam engine. Electric motors run washers, refrigerators, typewriters, fans, drills, and scores of other useful appliances.

Powerful electric motors have many uses in industry. They run elevators and hoists that lift heavy loads. They move assembly lines. Electric motors run trains, streetcars, and subways.

To make an armature take a brand new round (not hexagonal) pencil and saw off the brass ferule that holds the eraser. Sharpen both ends of the pencil. Obtain a small wooden sewing-thread spool. Saw and whittle square notches out of opposite sides of the spool. Push the pencil through the hole in the spool.

How can you make an electric motor?

Wind the armature in the following manner. Beginning about an inch from the end of a coil of No. 22 lacquered wire, wind three layers of wire lengthwise around the spool. Wind it closely, so that each turn touches the turn before and after itself. Cross over to the other side of the pencil to cover both surfaces of the notches. Be sure that you keep winding in the same direction. When you have finished, leave about an inch of wire. Secure this end of the wire by looping it into a simple knot at the end of the last turn.

Beneath the loose ends of the wire, cement two half-inch-wide strips of metal foil to the pencil so that each strip goes almost half way around the pencil, but does not touch on either side. Scrape the lacquer off the ends of the wire. Secure an end of the wire to each piece of metal foil, using adhesive or cellophane tape.

Drill a 5/16-inch hole part way into a block of wood that is 3½ inches long, 1¾ inches wide, and ¾ inch thick. Cut notches in the block as shown.

Obtain two iron bolts, 5/16 of an inch

HOW TO MAKE YOUR OWN ELECTRIC MOTOR

SPOOL

METAL FOIL

3 LAYERS OF #22 WIRE

in diameter and about 2½ inches long. Also obtain four metal washers that fit closely around the bolt. Place the washers on the bolt and then screw the bolt tightly into the hole in the block, leaving 1⅜ inches out of the hole. Repeat these steps using a second block of wood and the other bolt.

Starting one foot from the end of a coil of No. 22 lacquered wire, wind the wire closely around the bolt, beginning where the bolt enters the wood. Be sure that one washer is at each end of the bolt. Wind six tight layers of wire on the bolt. When you have finished winding, secure the wire with a simple loop knot. Leaving about 10 inches of wire free, continue winding on the other bolt, again beginning where the bolt enters the wood. However, now wind the wire in the direction opposite to that on the first bolt. Wind the wire twice around the notches in the wooden block and secure it with a simple loop knot. Leave a foot more, and then cut the wire. Lastly, wind around the notches of the first block the one foot piece of wire you left free at the begin-

ning and secure it with a loop knot. The bolts and block make up the stationary electromagnets of your motor.

Obtain two more wooden blocks, this time 3½ inches long, 1 inch wide, and ¾ inch thick. Drill a ⅛-inch hole a short way into each block. Each hole should be exactly as far from an end of a block as the bolt holes were from the ends of the other two blocks.

Using a wide, flat board for a base, affix to it the four blocks, as shown in the illustration. Use small wood screws that go through the base and into the bottoms of the blocks. Be sure that the ends of the bolts rest not more than an eighth of an inch from the armature. Place the pencil points of the armature in the empty holes in the blocks.

Cut from a coat hanger two straight

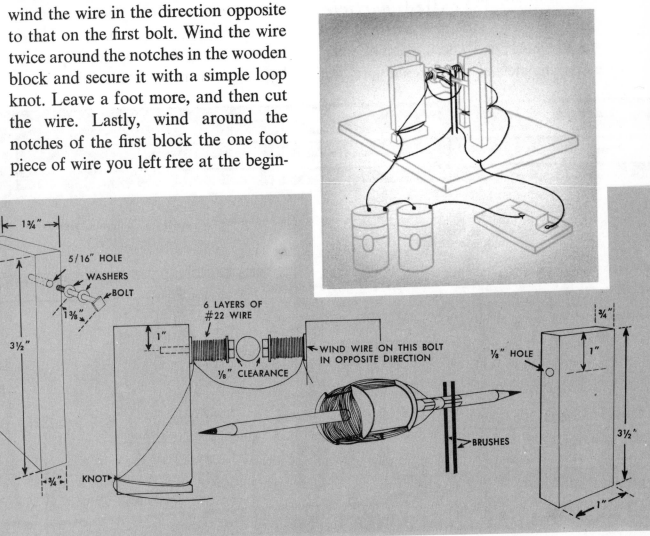

pieces of wire, each 3½ inches long. Place them upright in holes in the wooden base, so that they lightly touch the strips of metal foil on the pencil. The pieces of wire are your motor's brushes.

Connect wires to the brushes. Finally, connect all wires as shown in the illustration. Wherever wires connect, scrape off the lacquer. Two of the wires are run to a pair of dry cells that are connected.

If you have made the motor carefully, when you press down on your switch, the armature of the motor should begin to spin.

Among the most useful tools an atomic scientist has are huge machines called *particle accelerators*, or "atom smashers." These machines use electromagnets to give atomic particles

What part do magnets play in atomic research?

speeds almost as fast as light — almost 186,000 miles a second. One very important atom smasher is the *cyclotron*. A cyclotron consists of a large metal box, shaped like a pill box, located between the poles of a huge electromagnet. Air is removed from the box until a very high vacuum exists inside. Within the box there are two hollow, D-shaped half-circles of metal, called *dees*. These are given a very high electric charge that reverses itself millions of times a second. The atomic particles, perhaps protons, are fed into the cyclotron at the center of the dees. The electric charge on the atomic particle affects its magnetic field, and the big electromagnet either repels or attracts the particle. This causes the particle to begin to circle around within the dee. As it passes from one dee to another, the reversing electric charge reverses the charge on the dees. So, a particle that began to move because it was re-

The huge cyclotron at the University of California, Berkeley.

pelled when like magnetic poles acted upon one another, will not be pulled in the opposite direction when it moves into an area of unlike magnetic poles. The reversing electric field allows the particle to always be in a location where it will be repelled. As a result, the particle travels faster and faster in a spiral path until it reaches the outside wall of a dee. Here it shoots out of the cyclotron. The beam of very fast atomic particles shooting out of a cyclotron at targets of various materials enable scientists to learn very much about these materials and the particles that strike them.

Magnets In Communication

A telegraph is an apparatus for sending messages long distances over wires.

How are magnets used in a telegraph?

A telegraph circuit includes a sending key, a receiving sounder, and a source of electricity. The *sending key* is a switch that opens and closes the circuit. The important part of the sending key is a metal rod attached to a piece of springy metal. The rod has a button on one end. When the telegraph operator pushes down on this button, the rod makes contact with a small metal screw below it, and thereby closes an electric circuit. When the operator takes his finger off the button, the rod springs up and breaks the circuit.

The *sounder* has a lightweight magnetic metal bar, called an *armature,* suspended a fraction of an inch above the poles of an electromagnet. One end

TELEGRAPH

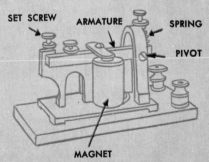

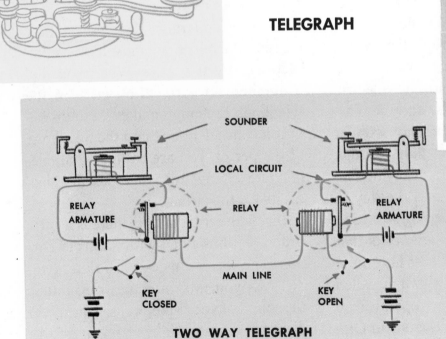

TWO WAY TELEGRAPH

At left, the diagram of a two way telegraph line with relays, as described on page 41 and 42.

of the armature is pivoted and has a spring pushing down on the upper part of the pivoted end. The other end is located between a second metal bar and a setscrew. When the telegraph operator pushes the sending key and makes a circuit, the electromagnet pulls one end of the armature suddenly downward. As the armature strikes the bar beneath it, a sharp click is heard. As soon as the operator releases the key, breaking the circuit, the electromagnet releases the end of the armature that it has pulled toward itself; the released end is pushed upward by the spring and strikes the set screw above with another sharp click.

Telegraph operators listen for the time between clicks. A short time (only about 1/5 of a second) is a *dot*. A longer time (about ½ a second) is a *dash*. By means of a code of combinations of dots and dashes, messages are sent along the wire that connects the key to a sounder.

Suppose a telegraph operator in Cincinnati wants to send a message to an operator in Tucson. The Cincinnati operator pushes his telegraph key down. This closes the circuit and electric current flows through the wires, the electromagnet in Tucson works, and the Tucson sounder clicks. You may wonder how electric current can flow through the wires when the telegraph key in Cincinnati is pushed down and the key in Tucson is open and keeping a circuit from being formed. The answer is that the operator in Tucson closes his end of the circuit by means of a switch called a *line switch*. When the operator in Tucson wants to answer the one in Cincinnati, the Tucson operator opens his line switch and the Cincinnati operator closes his.

In a telephone, electric current causes an electromagnet to attract a metal disc that makes a sound. Let us see how this happens.

How does a telephone work?

Sound is made when some object moves back and forth very rapidly in air. This back-and-forth movement is called *vibration*. When an object vibrates, it pushes air outward from itself in a series of waves. When these air waves strike our ears, we hear a sound. For example, when you hit a drum, it vibrates and causes sound waves to move through the air to your ears. The sound that comes from a telephone receiver is also caused by vibration.

The telephone has two main parts. One is the mouthpiece, or *transmitter*, and the other is the *receiver*. You speak into the mouthpiece and hold the receiver to your ear.

Like all apparatus that uses electric current, the telephone must have a complete electrical circuit. When you dial a number, an automatic switch in the telephone exchange makes a circuit between your telephone and the telephone of the person you are calling. The telephone exchange also supplies the electricity for the circuit.

Inside the transmitter, there is a little round, flat box filled with grains of carbon. The top of this box is a thin metal disc. As you talk into the transmitter, the sound of your voice causes the metal disc to vibrate. The back-and-forth

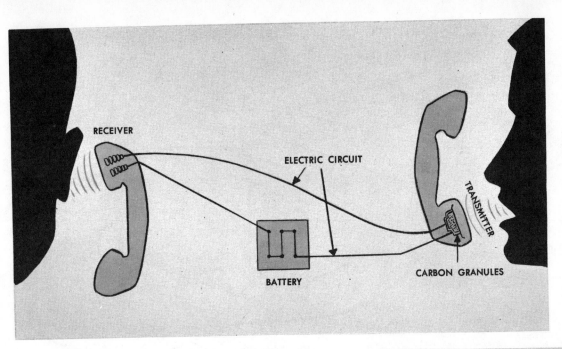

RECEIVER

ELECTRIC CIRCUIT

TRANSMITTER

CARBON GRANULES

BATTERY

Left, a simple telephone circuit with a battery. Below, a cutaway view of the telephone receiver showing the position of armature, permanent magnet, and electromagnet.

(After diagrams, courtesy Bell Telephone Laboratories.)

movement of the disc alternately presses the carbon grains together and then leaves them room to spread apart.

The grains of carbon are part of the electric circuit. Electricity can pass through the carbon grains more easily when they are pressed together than when they are spread apart. For this reason, the amount of electricity that passes the carbon grains changes from moment to moment as the disc vibrates.

This changing electric current passes along the wire to the receiver. In the receiver are an electromagnet and a metal disc. As the changing amount of electricity passes along the wire to the receiver, the electromagnet's pull varies from strong to weak. When the pull is strong, the disc is moved toward the electromagnet, and when the pull is weak, the disc springs away from the electromagnet. This back-and-forth movement of the disc causes air in front of the receiver to move back and forth in the same way. The vibrations of the disc cause sound waves to reach the ear that is held to the receiver. The sounds made by the receiver are the same as

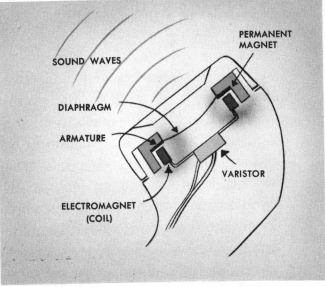

SOUND WAVES

PERMANENT MAGNET

DIAPHRAGM

ARMATURE

VARISTOR

ELECTROMAGNET (COIL)

those made by the voice at the other end of the wire.

The important thing to remember about a telephone is that it is not sound that travels along the wires. It is a changing amount of electricity that is caused by sound at the transmitter and is changed to sound by the receiver.

Using wood and small nails, build a wooden frame like the one in the illustration.

How can you make a telegraph set?

Before putting the frame together, ham-

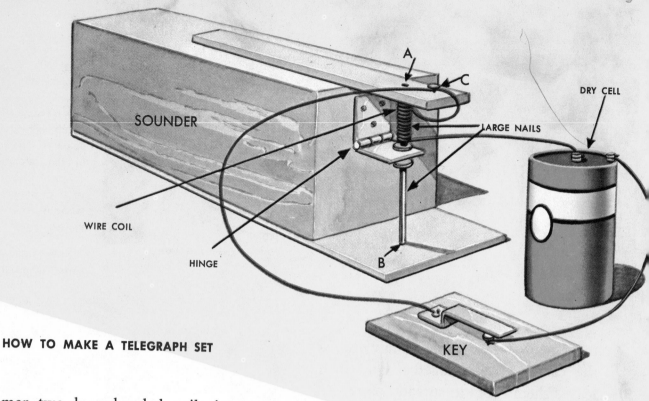

SOUNDER

A

C

DRY CELL

LARGE NAILS

WIRE COIL

HINGE

B

KEY

HOW TO MAKE A TELEGRAPH SET

mer two large-headed nails into two of the pieces of wood at the points marked A and B in the illustration, and a small nail at C. The two nails must be in a straight line, and their heads must be only one-fourth of an inch apart. Wind a coil of wire in two or three layers around the upper nail and keep the wire in place with adhesive tape. Attach one end of the wire to one binding-post of a dry cell. Drive a small nail almost all the way into the top of the wooden frame. Attach to this nail the other end of the wire from the coil. Be sure to scrape the insulation off the ends of the wires before making connections.

Obtain a steel hinge Make sure the hinge swings easily. If it doesn't, put a drop of oil into the cracks where the two halves of the hinge meet. Slip one half of the hinge between the heads of the two nails, as in the illustration. Nail or screw the other half of the hinge to the wooden frame, so that the unattached half of the hinge can move easily up and down. (It may be easier to do this before you put the frame together.) This completes your sounder.

Connect two long wires to the switch you have been using in your experiments. The switch is now your telegraph key. Connect one of the wires to the nail on the top of the sounder. Connect the other wire to the second binding post of the dry cell. Your telegraph is complete.

Push the switch down and immediately let it up. The result is two clicks — one when the hinge flew up to hit the electromagnet (the upper nail) and the other when it fell back to the lower nail. By holding the switch down for a shorter or longer time, you can telegraph dots and dashes. By using the Morse code shown on page 45, you can telegraph messages.

MORSE CODE

A · −		R · − ·
B − · · ·	J · − − −	S · · ·
C − · − ·	K − · −	T −
D − · ·	L · − · ·	U · · −
E ·	M − −	V · · · −
F · · − ·	N − ·	W · − −
G − − ·	O − − −	X − · · −
H · · · ·	P · − − ·	Y − · − −
I · ·	Q − − · −	Z − − · ·

How can you make a simple telephone? You will need the carbon rod from the center of a dead dry cell, the carbon rod from the center of a flashlight battery, a cigar box, a live dry cell, wires and an old telephone receiver or a set of earphones. Saw off two one-inch lengths of the carbon rod from the dead dry cell, and grind out a small hollow in the end of each piece. With sandpaper, sharpen the ends of the rod from the flashlight battery. Affix the two hollowed-out pieces of carbon to the back of the cigar box, using wire in the manner shown. The sharpened carbon rod should be placed between the two pieces of carbon, so that its points touch the hollowed-out place in each piece. Fasten a long piece of bell wire to each of the hollowed-out pieces of carbon, and run one wire to one pole of the live dry cell. Run the other wire to another room, where you connect it to the telephone

HOW TO MAKE A SIMPLE TELEPHONE

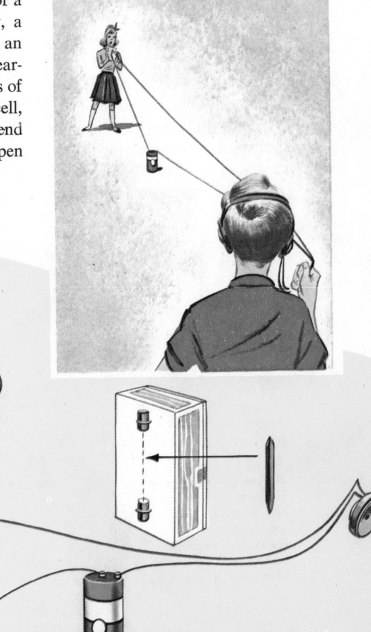

WOODEN CIGAR BOX

CARBON ROD

CARBON ROD

WIRE

DRY CELL

EAR PHONES

CARBON ROD FROM FLASHLIGHT BATTERY

receiver or headphones. Take a third wire and connect the other pole of the dry cell with the receiver, as the illustration shows. Your telephone is complete. If someone talks into the front of the cigar box, the movement of the sharpened carbon rod will vary the amount of electric current in the wires, and the diaphragm of the receiver will vibrate to produce the same sound waves as those of the person speaking into the box.

We learned that an electric current in

What part do magnets play in radio and television?

a wire produces a magnetic field. If the amount of current is varied, the strength of the field varies. If you have the proper electronic apparatus, you can broadcast the variations of the magnetic field. This is exactly what is done in radio and television broadcasting. The broadcast variations are called *electromagnetic waves*. The electronic equipment in radio and television sets can detect the electromagnetic waves at long distances from where they are broadcast. Let us see how this works.

A microphone in a broadcasting studio is much like a transmitter in a telephone. Sound waves enter the microphone and cause it to vary the strength of electrical impulses. These impulses produce magnetic fields of varying strength, and the variations are broadcast as electromagnetic waves that we call radio waves. When these electromagnetic waves reach a radio, electronic equipment changes them into electric current of varying strength. This varying electric current varies the strength of an electromagnet that moves a diaphragm. The movements of the diaphragm are changed into sound just

Did you ever realize how important a part magnets and magnetism play in radio and TV broadcasting and receiving, tape recording, and the making of phonograph records?

as in a telephone receiver. So, you can see that the "sound" that is broadcast to a radio receiver is really a series of electromagnetic waves that are changed into sound by the action of an electromagnet. A television set has a radio inside its cabinet to reproduce sounds broadcast from the television studio.

A television picture also depends on magnets. When a television camera focuses on an object, light reflected from the object enters the lens of the camera and falls on a screen, which is inside a large glass tube. Also inside the tube is an electron gun that shoots a moving beam of electrons at the screen. The beam sweeps back and forth across the screen from top to bottom, 30 times a second. This is called *scanning*. The path of the moving beam is controlled by electromagnets. The beam is affected differently by the light and dark areas on the screen across which it sweeps.

These differences are changed into varying electromagnetic waves that are then broadcast.

The television receiver in your home has a large electronic tube something like the one in the television camera. It, too, has a magnetically-controlled electron gun and scans a screen in the tube. Actually, two electron beams scan the screen, each making 525 separate horizontal lines 30 times a second. You surely have seen these light and dark lines on the screen of your television set. The screen is at the front of the tube and is made of a chemical substance that glows more or less brightly, depending on the strength of the electron beam that strikes it. The variations in brightness match the variations in light that enter the television camera. As a result, the picture on your television screen matches the objects on which the television camera is focused.

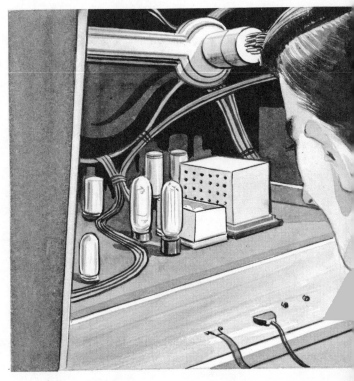

You and Magnetism

No one yet knows how to relate the effects of magnetism with other scientific knowledge and thus clarify its basic nature, but physicists are already engaged in numerous projects and experiments, seeking such a connection, trying to find out exactly why magnetism exerts a force and why it seems to exist at all known parts of the universe. At the National Magnet Laboratory (supervised by the Massachusetts Institute of Technology) in Boston a magnet has sustained for about a minute a magnetic field 500,000 times stronger than the earth's and produced pressure greater than that found in the deepest seas. The development of superconducting magnets — electromagnets maintained by current in superconductors — could in time make possible astonishing miniaturization, such as compressing the working parts of a room-size computer into a unit about the size of a portable TV set.

In many countries, now, electricity is being generated by atomic reactors. The fuel to run these machines is obtained from the rare chemical element, uranium. A much better, cheaper way to tap tremendous energy would be to harness the power of the hydrogen bomb, but to do this, an extremely hot gas called a *plasma* is used. Since no material can hold anything as hot as plasma, scientists are attempting to hold it in a magnetic bottle — a bottle-shaped magnetic field. So far, magnetic bottles have been able to contain it for only a few thousandths of a second. Perhaps *you* will be the one to devise a magnetic bottle that can hold plasma for an indefinite time, making possible cheap and safe atomic energy that will generate electricity for remote areas.

So far, magnetic bottles have been able to hold the plasma for only a few thousandths of a second.

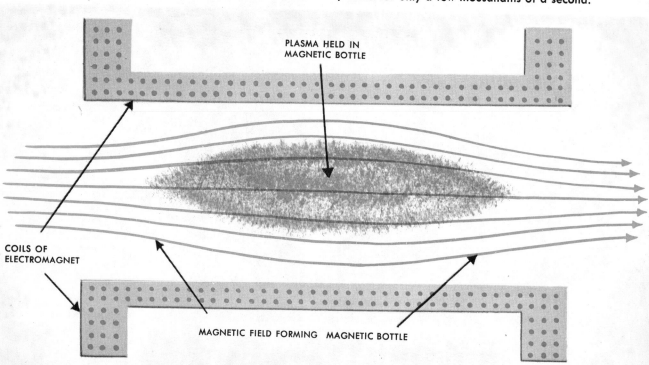

PLASMA HELD IN
MAGNETIC BOTTLE

COILS OF
ELECTROMAGNET

MAGNETIC FIELD FORMING MAGNETIC BOTTLE

THE HOW AND WHY WONDER BOOK OF
ELECTRICITY

By Jerome J. Notkin, Ed. D., Science Supervisor, Suffolk County, N.Y.
and Sidney Gulkin, M.S. in Ed., Teacher, New York City

Illustrated by Robert Patterson and Charles Bernard

Edited under the supervision of
 Dr. Paul E. Blackwood,
 Washington, D. C.

Text and illustrations approved by
 Oakes A. White, Brooklyn Children's Museum, Brooklyn, New York

GROSSET & DUNLAP • **Publishers** • **NEW YORK**

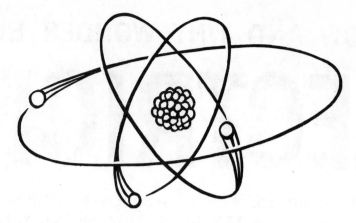

INTRODUCTION

When a town stands still for eight hours, it is missing something mighty important. One such town stood still because the electricity stopped. This was most inconvenient for everyone, but it did make a boy named Mike and his sister Susan Jane think about it. They were filled with questions: What is electricity? How do we make electricity? How does electricity get to our town?

Just as Mike and his sister explore the wonders of electricity with their father, so will inquisitive children everywhere get answers to their questions about electricity as they read this book. Like the others in the *How and Why Wonder Book* series, this science book is authentic and colorful and can be read with interest by the whole family.

The answers to questions about electricity that are now easy to give young people are the answers which stretched the minds of the greatest scientists less than a hundred years ago. Fortunately, books give children the wealth of information which took so long for scientists to discover.

Thinking, investigating and experimenting are the special paths which are basic to science. This book, which includes more than a dozen experiments to help readers discover what others have found before, will lead children along these same paths. It is an excellent addition to the school or home collection of science books for young readers and their parents.

Paul E. Blackwood

Dr. Blackwood is a professional employee in the U. S. Office of Education. This book was edited by him in his private capacity and no official support or endorsement by the Office of Education is intended or should be inferred.

CONTENTS

Page

THE DAY THE TOWN STOOD STILL

Why is the main electrical cable the lifeline of a modern industrial town? 4

How are we dependent upon electricity? 5

WHAT IS THIS MAGICAL THING CALLED ELECTRICITY?

In what ways does a waterfall serve us? 6

What are some of the ways we know of to make electricity? 7

What kind of power is used to run subways? 8

What makes the generator spin around? 9

What part does the steam play in this experiment? 10

In what way are electrons pushed? 10

Why is a cell called a portable power station? 11

HIGHWAYS THAT CARRY ELECTRICITY

How does a transformer help us get electricity to our homes? 12

Why is copper most commonly used for electrical wiring? 14

Why don't we use copper wires in our toaster? 14

Can you name three electrical things in your home that use poor conductors? 14

ELECTRICITY IS REALLY A FIRST COUSIN OF MAGNETS

Are magnets and electricity related? 15

What happens when electricity flows through a wire? 17

What happens when a magnet moves inside a coil of wire? 18

How is a switch like a door? 18

ELECTRICITY NEEDS TRANSFORMERS

Why is your toy train transformer called a step-down transformer? 19

What does a step-up transformer do? 20

WE MUST OBSERVE SAFETY RULES

Can you remember at least five "never" rules? 21

DRY CELLS ARE THE SAFE WAY

Why should we never place a piece of metal across the two terminals? 25

Page

In how many ways can we use dry cells? 25

Can you name some of the parts of a dry cell? 26

Why is it called a dry cell? 26

Why is a storage battery called a "battery" and not a "cell"? 26

What are the two liquids used in a storage battery? 27

Why does the storage battery use distilled water? 27

THE POLICEMAN OF THE HIGHWAYS

How does the overflow valve in the automobile protect it? 28

Why is the fuse often called the twenty-four-hour policeman? 29

ACTIVITIES FOR JUNIOR ELECTRICIANS

No. 1. How does your flashlight work? 30

No. 2. How can a switch help us? 31

No. 3. How can we connect two dry cells to give us more power than one cell? 32

No. 4. How can we connect two dry cells to make them last longer? 33

No. 5. How can we connect several light bulbs in series? 34

No. 6. How can we connect several light bulbs in parallel? 35

No. 7. How can we find out which objects are good conductors? 36

No. 8. How can we make a quiz board? 37

No. 9. How does a fuse protect us? 38

No. 10. How can we make an electromagnet? 39

No. 11. How can we make an electromagnet stronger? 40

No. 12. How can we make an electromagnet stronger in another way? 41

No. 13. How can we make a telegraph set? 42

No. 14. How can we make an electric current detector? 43

SUMMARY OF IMPORTANT IDEAS 44

SOME IMPORTANT TERMS FOR YOU TO REMEMBER 46

SOME FAMOUS SCIENTISTS WHO MADE THE ELECTRICAL AGE POSSIBLE 48

THE DAY THE TOWN STOOD STILL

Why is the main electrical cable the lifeline of a modern industrial town?

THIS story is not made up. It is true. It really happened. My town stood still for eight hours. Why? We had no electricity.

My house was not the same. The bells didn't ring. My mother's washing machine stopped dead. Our television set was dark and silent. The little radio in my room was just a box without a voice. Our electric stove joined the washing machine, radio, and refrigerator. The electric clock in the kitchen was stopped at 10:36 A.M. That's when it happened. Mother changed the fuses. That was no help.

Our neighbor came running to us for help. Nothing was working in her house, either. She was really worried. Her baby's formula needed refrigeration. The food was becoming spoiled. She tried to call the doctor for her sick baby. But her phone was not working either.

My mother drove her in the car to pick up the doctor. When she arrived at the gas station to fill up the tank she was told that the pumps were not working. Several cars were stuck in the middle of the road. No gas!

Then mother turned the car radio on. It worked! It worked on the storage battery. The radio was full of news.

"Main cable at the power station destroyed by explosion. . . . Repairs are under way, but it will take at least eight hours. . . . Motorists are urged to give help to those who need it most."

So that was it! The main electrical cable had been damaged.

"Why is that cable so important?" I asked my mother.

"That cable is like the main pipe supplying us with water, Mike," my mother replied. "When that pipe is broken, the water stops running. There is just no other way of getting water. And there is no other way of getting electrical power until that cable is repaired."

How are we dependent upon electricity?

By the time Dad came home it was dark. We helped him get into the house by flashlight. We had two candles — one in the kitchen, another in the living room.

We had our cold dinner by candlelight. My sister, Susan Jane, and I had a lot of fun, but Mother and Dad didn't think it was so funny.

The people on my street walked about with flashlights, knocking on each others' doors instead of ringing doorbells.

Everyone was excited.

"When will the lights go on?" people asked.

"Soon, soon," my Dad replied.

It seemed that a long time passed before the lights suddenly came on. The buzz of the refrigerator started. My little radio was on at full volume. The television set suddenly came to life with picture and sound.

It seemed as if the sun had suddenly begun to shine in the middle of the night.

My town began to move again!

5

WHAT IS THIS MAGICAL THING CALLED ELECTRICITY?

In what ways does a waterfall serve us?

"ELECTRICITY, or electrical power, just doesn't happen," said Dad. "It has to be made. How? What things are used to make it? Let's see.

"When my grandfather ground his wheat," said Dad, "he had to take it to a mill that was near a waterfall."

"Why near a waterfall?" I asked.

"Well, Mike," said Dad, "they used the waterfall for the power to run the mill. If you have never seen one, or don't know how it works, we can build a model. We need a cheese box, a stick for an axle or shaft, and some jar covers for blades.

"When water falls on these covers or blades, the shaft goes around, and it, in turn, moves wheels and gears. You see, then, that the fuel used to turn these wheels is free. The water moves the blades and the mill is in business."

"That's terrific, Dad, but how does falling water make electricity?" I asked.

THIS IS A HYDROELECTRIC DAM RUN BY WATER POWER, OR THE FORCE CAUSED BY THE DIFFERENCE IN ELEVATION OF THE WATER BEHIND AND BELOW THE DAM. WATER POWER MAY BE DESCRIBED AS THE POWER OF WATER USED TO MOVE OR DRIVE A MACHINE. THE FLOW OF WATER IN RIVERS AND STREAMS IS A SOURCE OF ENERGY. WHEN THE WATER, WHICH HAS BEEN COLLECTING BEHIND THE DAM, RUSHES DOWN, THIS ENERGY TURNS THE GENERATOR AND PRODUCES ELECTRICITY.

What are some of the ways we know of to make electricity?

"To make electricity which will not only turn a mill, but send out the electrons through roads made of wire, shafts have to be turned inside a tunnel, called a generator or dynamo. Water very often supplies the power to turn the shafts that make or generate this magical electricity."

"Oh, yes. We learned about some of these places in school. There is Hoover Dam, Niagara Falls, the dams of the Tennessee Valley Authority, Grand Coulee and Bonneville dams, and many others like them."

"Very good, Mike," smiled Dad. "And power from these places is sent hundreds of miles to homes, factories, farms and schools. It even runs railroads and subways."

"Really, Dad? Can water power do all that? But suppose there are no waterfalls or dams nearby?"

THERE ARE DIFFERENT KINDS OF POWER PLANTS, BUT THEY ALL HAVE SOMETHING IN COMMON. EACH POWER PLANT HAS A GENERATOR WHERE ELECTRICITY IS MADE. THIS IS A COAL-BURNING POWER PLANT. WATER IS HEATED BY A COAL FIRE AND STEAM MAKES THE GENERATOR MOVE.

What kind of power is used to run subways?

"The scientists and engineers have thought about that. They have figured out ways to make electricity from other things. Take coal as an example. That can help make electricity for use anywhere. Do you know that subways in many of our large cities run on coal-made electricity?"

"That's real magic!" said my sister, who had been listening quietly all along.

"No, Susan Jane, I wouldn't say it is magic. I like to call it science. It can be explained and used by everyone, not only by magicians."

"Does it work like the dams?" Susan Jane asked.

"Something like it," Dad continued. "In the case of dams, water goes into a pipe where it turns the blades of the large wheels. Coal is often used to heat water and convert it into steam which goes into the pipes. The large wheels are called turbines."

GENERATOR

TURBINE

"Is this turbine connected to anything?" I asked.

"Oh, yes. It's the turbine that makes the generator spin around. Electricity comes out the other side."

Susan Jane looked puzzled. She asked, "What is a generator? What does it do? How does it work?"

"I'll show you," said Dad. "We can make a model of a generator. But we'll need some things. Susan Jane, bring Mother's teakettle. Mike, bring your magnet and your flashlight. I have the other things we need."

9

What part does the steam play in this experiment? Susan Jane and I ran to get these things, wondering how the kettle was going to be used.

"Now, then," said Dad when we returned, "watch and you will see how a generator makes electricity. The fire heats the water in the kettle. That makes the steam, just as burning coal can boil water to make steam. It is this steam power that pushes against the blades of the turbine. My turbine is made of cardboard, but it gives you the idea. Then the turbine turns the magnet inside a coil of electrical wire."

"Is a magnet really used?" I asked.

In what way are electrons pushed? "Yes. It is a magnet made by electricity, called an electromagnet. There are many turns of covered wire wound around an iron core. As the magnet moves inside a coil of wire, it pushes tiny things called electrons. When electrons are pushed or moved, electricity flows. That is why the light bulb that I removed from your flashlight goes on."

"Gosh, Dad, just think — a magnet and a wire make our television sets work!" I said.

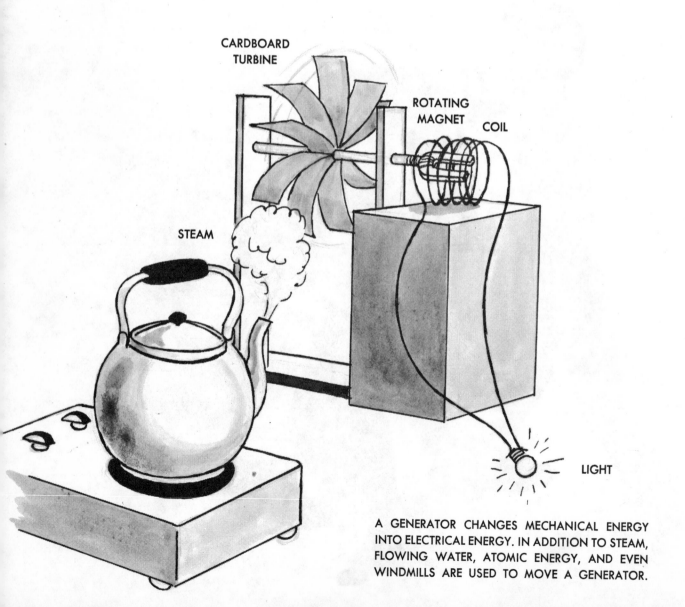

CARDBOARD TURBINE

ROTATING MAGNET COIL

STEAM

LIGHT

A GENERATOR CHANGES MECHANICAL ENERGY INTO ELECTRICAL ENERGY. IN ADDITION TO STEAM, FLOWING WATER, ATOMIC ENERGY, AND EVEN WINDMILLS ARE USED TO MOVE A GENERATOR.

"Right, Mike. But remember, it is not this toy magnet and not this small piece of wire. It is a large electromagnet turning inside a huge coil of wire. It looks more like a tunnel. The more wire in the coil, the more electrons can be moved. And we get more electricity.

Why is a cell called a portable power station?

"Do you mean that my flashlight and portable radio carry a generator inside of them just for me, every time I want to use it?" I asked, looking at my flashlight.

"That's right. The battery is its own power station."

YOUR PORTABLE POWER STATION

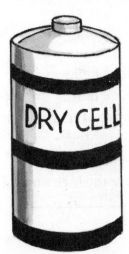

DRY CELL

POWER
STATION

TRANSFORMER

HIGHWAYS THAT CARRY ELECTRICITY

How does a transformer help us get electricity to our homes?

"HOW DO these electrons travel all the way from the power station to us?" I wanted to know.

"I was coming to that. Do you know that as we ride along the highways there are electrical highways right above our heads that we hardly ever notice? Sometimes they are even under the roads."

"What are they for?" Susan Jane asked.

"They are the highways of wire where those invisible electrons are flowing toward homes, factories and farms," Dad answered. "The electricity has to be delivered where it is needed and in the right amount. Instead of trucks and trains that carry off goods from factories, wire or cables do the job here. They do it quietly, without any fuss."

"How do the wires do it?" asked my sister.

"Well, all along the roads where the electricity is carried are devices called transformers. They change electric current from a high to a low voltage, or the reverse, and allow the wires to carry more electrical current."

SUB-STATION

TRANSFORMER

TRANSFORMERS

ELECTRICITY FROM THE POWER STATION IS CARRIED THROUGH WIRES TO HOMES, FAC-
TORIES, STORES, FARMS AND SCHOOLS. TRANSFORMERS HELP IN THE TRANSPORTATION
OF ELECTRICITY FROM THE POWER STATION TO ALL THESE PLACES. A TRANSFORMER IS
A MACHINE THAT TRANSFORMS OR CHANGES AN ELECTRIC CURRENT FROM A HIGH TO
A LOW VOLTAGE. IT CAN ALSO CHANGE CURRENT FROM A LOW TO A HIGH VOLTAGE.
THE TEXT AND ILLUSTRATIONS BEGINNING ON PAGE 19 WILL FURTHER EXPLAIN THE
FUNCTION OF A TRANSFORMER.

Why is copper most commonly used for electrical wiring?

"The wires or cables are made of material that must be a good conductor or carrier. It's like having a good clear road without bumps and rocks for cars to travel over. Good conductors are usually made of copper."

"Is copper the only conductor of electricity?" I asked.

"No. There are other ones. Silver is the best, but it's too expensive to use. Aluminum is also a good conductor and is gaining wider use because of its lightness. We use millions of tons of copper to make electrical wire for all purposes."

Why don't we use copper wires in our toaster?

"Do we always use copper?" Susan Jane wanted to know.

"No," said Dad. "Take our toaster, for example. The curled-up wires inside of it happen to be poor conductors."

"Wouldn't that mean that when electricity tries to get through, it will have a tough job?" I asked. I was puzzled.

Dad smiled. "What happens in a toaster? The wires get red hot. This shows us that electricity is having a difficult job passing through. But it makes our toast taste good. In an electric stove it broils our steaks and chops and cooks our meals. That's not all. Mother's electric iron uses these poor conductors or carriers, too. Otherwise the flat bottom of the iron would not get hot enough to iron our shirts, tablecloths and other things.

Can you name three electrical things in your home that use poor conductors?

"There are many other uses for these poor conductors. Can you name some other appliances which might have them?"

"Heating pads."

"Coffee makers."

"Waffle irons."

"An electric heater."

"An electric frying pan."

"That's enough," laughed Dad. "Now let's ask Mother to put electricity to work and prepare some lunch. This talk about steak and chops is making me hungry."

"Me, too," we echoed, and everyone went into the kitchen.

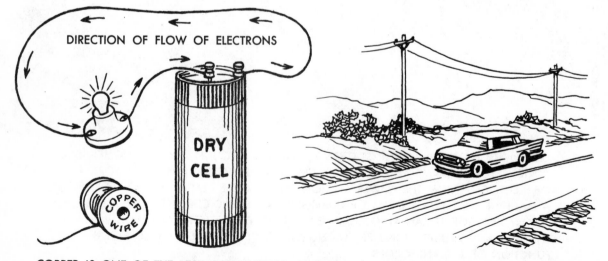

DIRECTION OF FLOW OF ELECTRONS

DRY CELL

COPPER WIRE

COPPER IS ONE OF THE BEST CONDUCTORS OF ELECTRIC CURRENT, AND IT IS USED WIDELY IN THE MANUFACTURE OF THIN ELECTRICAL WIRE, AS WELL AS THE HEAVIER CABLES ALONG HIGHWAYS.

ELECTRICITY IS REALLY A FIRST COUSIN OF MAGNETS

Are magnets and electricity related?

"YOU know, Dad, one of the things that you said yesterday still confuses me. What does the electrical magnet have to do with making electricity? I know that magnets have some kind of power. They can attract nails and other things. But how do magnets help us make electricity?"

While I was talking, Susan Jane was picking things up with my magnet.

"Magnets and electricity are in the same family," explained Dad. "We might even say they are cousins. We can try something to clear this up."

MAGNETS HAVE A DRAWING OR PULLING POWER, AND ATTRACT THINGS MADE OF STEEL, IRON AND NICKEL.

THE WORD *MAGNETISM* COMES FROM THE NAME *MAGNESIA*, AN ANCIENT CITY OF ASIA, WHERE MANY LOADSTONES WERE FOUND. THE LOADSTONE, ALSO SPELLED LODESTONE, IS A MAGNETIC ROCK, AND WAS USED BY ANCIENT PEOPLES IN THE SAILING OF SHIPS. LIKE A COMPASS NEEDLE, A PIECE OF LOADSTONE ROCK WILL POINT NORTH.

"Can we help?" begged Susan Jane.

"Why, sure. Mike, bring down your scout compass. Susan Jane, bring the cover of your crayon box."

When we returned, Dad had removed the dry cell from my flashlight.

"Put the compass into the cover," Dad instructed. "Wind some insulated wire about eight or ten times around the cover."

What happens when electricity flows through a wire?

Then Dad touched one end of the wire, which had been stripped back, to the bottom of the dry cell, and he touched the other end to the center part at the top of the cell.

"Did you see what happened?" asked Dad.

"Yes, the needle of Mike's compass moved."

"That's right. You know that one magnet can move another magnet. When electricity went through the wire, the needle, which is a magnet, moved. That means that, somewhere, there was another magnet. When electricity flows through wires, there is magnetism around the wires."

"Can we see it?" asked Susan Jane.

"No. Not any more than we can see magnetism pulling nails to Mike's magnet. But the magnetism is there, all right."

"I'm not sure I understand," I said.

HANS CHRISTIAN OERSTED DISCOVERED THAT ELECTRICITY AND MAGNETISM WERE RELATED. IN THE YEAR 1820, OERSTED OBSERVED THAT WHEN HE SENT AN ELECTRIC CURRENT THROUGH A WIRE THAT WAS NEAR A COMPASS, THE COMPASS NEEDLE MOVED. HE SHOWED THAT THE FLOW OF ELECTRICITY THROUGH A WIRE CAUSES A MAGNETISM AROUND THE WIRE. MICHAEL FARADAY ALSO EXPERIMENTED WITH ELECTRICITY AND MAGNETISM. HIS IMPORTANT WORK RESULTED IN THE FIRST ELECTRIC GENERATOR.

What happens when a magnet moves inside a coil of wire?

"You will soon, Mike. If a magnet moves when electrons go through a coil of wire, would electrons move when a magnet passes through a coil? This puzzled a scientist several hundred years ago, and he decided to experiment. His experiment worked, and that marked the beginning of many wonderful things.

"If we use a small magnet and a small wire, only a few electrons would move. But when we move very powerful magnets inside thousands of coils, many electrons flow. It doesn't matter whether the magnets or the coils move, but it's the movement which generates the electricity."

"I understand it more clearly now, Dad."

"Good. As you see, there's nothing magical about it," said Dad. "But let's back up a bit. Do you remember that I kept tapping one end of the wire to the dry cell to make the compass move? We can do it easier if we use a switch, such as we have in our house."

"Does it make any difference if it's an up-and-down switch or one that we use to ring the doorbell?" asked Susan Jane.

How is a switch like a door?

"Not one bit," answered Dad. "Each one can turn something on and off. When we close any switch, the connection is completed and the electrons can flow again. When we open the switch, the connection is broken and the electrons cannot flow."

Susan Jane exclaimed, "That's just like opening or closing a gate or door."

"Of course! That's a nice way to put it," complimented Dad. "Did you ever hear the expression, 'completing the circuit' or 'breaking the circuit'? That's what is meant. When the switch is closed, the light, the refrigerator, the waffle iron, the coffee maker, and your electric train, all go on. When we turn the switch off, these appliances go off."

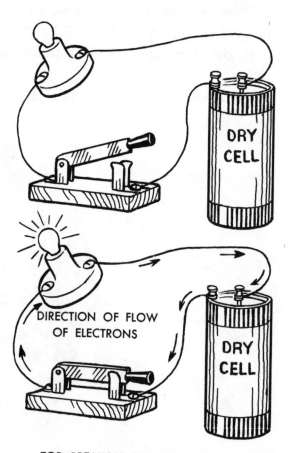

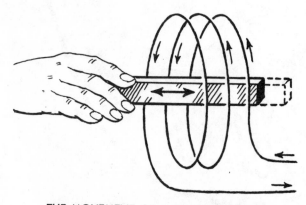

THE MOVEMENT OF A MAGNET INSIDE A COIL OF WIRE GENERATES ELECTRICITY.

TOP: BREAKING THE CIRCUIT.
BOTTOM: COMPLETING THE CIRCUIT.

18

IRON CORE

OUR HOMES ARE OFTEN SUPPLIED WITH 110 VOLTS OF ELECTRICITY, BUT TOY ELECTRIC TRAINS, FOR EXAMPLE, NEED FEWER VOLTS TO OPERATE. STEP-DOWN TRANSFORMERS STEP DOWN, OR DE-CREASE, THE VOLTAGE OF AN ALTERNATING CURRENT, ENABLING A TOY TRAIN TO RUN.

50 TURNS

5 TURNS

11 VOLTS A.C.
TO RUN TOY TRAIN →

→ 110 VOLTS A.C.

ELECTRICITY NEEDS TRANSFORMERS

Why is your toy train transformer called a step-down transformer?

"DOESN'T the train set you gave me for my birthday work from my transformer? I never really knew what that word meant," I said.

"Let's look it up in the dictionary," suggested Susan Jane.

"A good idea," said Dad. "Let's see. Transform means, 'to change in form.'

"When we use a transformer for a train, we plug it into the wall socket. Our home is supplied with 110 volts of electricity. Our train uses much less, perhaps eight to twelve volts. How can we cut it down?"

"Does the transformer do the job for us?" I wanted to know.

"Yes, it does. It steps it down, just as it does in other parts of the house. We have a transformer to step down the voltage before it goes into our doorbell. We could use batteries, too, but we'd have to replace them when they were used up."

"How does a transformer work?" Susan Jane asked.

"Very simply, it works like this," said Dad. "There are two coils of wire, one larger than the other. If current is sent through the first coil, magnetism surrounds it. The second coil is affected by the magnetism and electricity comes out of its wires.

"If the second coil is larger than the first coil, higher voltage comes out than went into the original coil. If the second coil is smaller, as in your train set, less voltage comes out.

"The transformer raises or lowers the voltage of the current. We can step it up or step it down.

"Remember, when we speak of current, we mean A.C., or alternating current. Dry cells and storage batteries are all D.C., or direct current."

"Are these transformers used only in toy trains and in doorbells?" inquired Susan Jane.

"No. Their most important use is in changing the voltage of electricity from the power station, a steam-turbine, hydroelectric, or atomic power plant, to places many miles away.

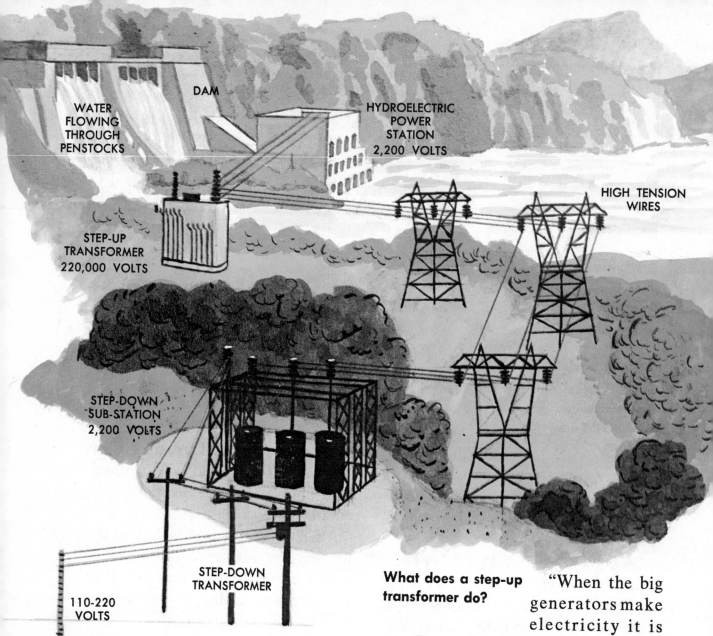

DAM

WATER
FLOWING
THROUGH
PENSTOCKS

HYDROELECTRIC
POWER
STATION
2,200 VOLTS

HIGH TENSION
WIRES

STEP-UP
TRANSFORMER
220,000 VOLTS

STEP-DOWN
SUB-STATION
2,200 VOLTS

STEP-DOWN
TRANSFORMER

110-220
VOLTS

FUSE
BOX

OUTLET

TRAIN
TRANSFORMER

8-12 VOLTS

What does a step-up transformer do? "When the big generators make electricity it is usually at about 2,200 volts pressure. Step-up transformers raise the pressure about 100 times, to around 220,000 volts. This helps it travel along the wires better. When it gets near the place where it is wanted, step-down transformers lower it back to 2,200 volts. Before it reaches our home, another step-down transformer lowers it to 110 volts. In some homes, 220 volts are used.

"As you see, these wonderful machines increase pressure or voltage. They also act as shrinkers of voltage."

WE MUST OBSERVE SAFETY RULES

"DO YOU remember when I had my arm in a sling? That was a very bad burn I received as a result of carelessness with electricity," Dad told us.

"How did it happen?" Susan Jane wanted to know.

"I tried to plug in my electric razor while my hands were wet," Dad explained. "I am pretty lucky to be alive. I was so badly burned that the doctor had to treat me for several weeks before I could use my hand.

Can you remember at least five "never" rules?

"If you really want to have fun with electricity," said Dad, "you must first learn to play the important game of NEVER."

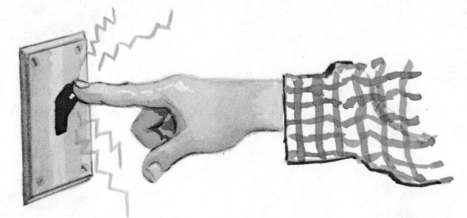

NEVER touch a switch with wet or damp hands. Water is a conductor. You might be badly burned or receive a severe shock. When you touch a switch, or any electric appliance, be sure your hands are dry.

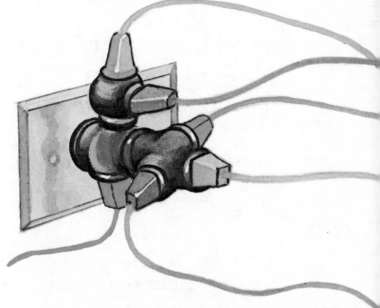

NEVER overload your connections. Don't try to plug too many electric appliances into one home appliance circuit. It is dangerous and can cause a short circuit or fire.

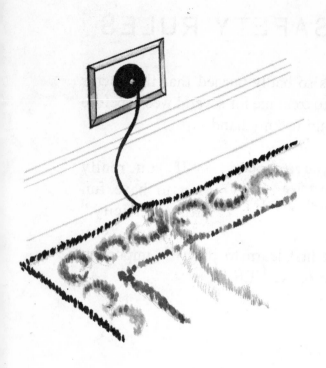

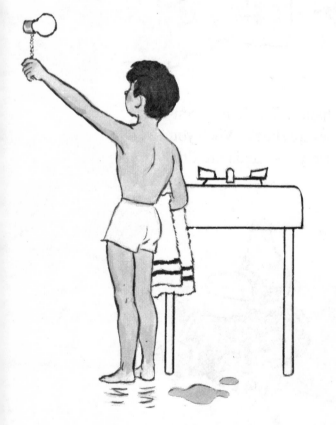

NEVER put electrical wires under carpets and rugs.

NEVER put a penny in the fuse box. Use the proper-sized fuse.

NEVER pull the chain of a light bulb if you are standing on a wet floor.

NEVER poke around the radio or television set if the switch is on.

NEVER touch an electrical appliance, switch, radio, or television set while bathing or when wet.

NEVER remain under or near a tree during an electrical storm or thunderstorm. Lightning may strike it.

NEVER remain in a lake during a thunderstorm.

NEVER, but never, touch a broken cable after or during a storm, or at any time. Call a policeman or fireman.

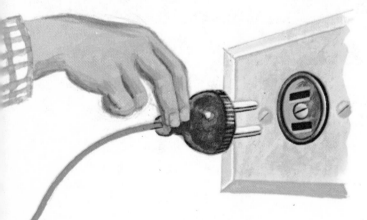

NEVER place anything except a plug into a wall socket.

"Remember," continued Dad as we listened very carefully, "electricity can be your friend or your enemy. You cannot argue with it. It will not forgive your mistakes. It will not accept your apology. It will reward you or punish you. It does not play favorites. Treat it with respect and understanding and it will serve you loyally."

DRY CELLS ARE THE SAFE WAY

D AD walked over to us and placed his hands on our shoulders. "Well, if you follow these NEVER rules, you will be doing the right thing. You can still have lots of fun with electricity if you work with dry cells. They cost little and you can carry them with you. You can put them in a box and take them to school, to the playground, to your friend's home or porch, and perform experiments. You can have a grand time. They are useful and safe."

Why should we never place a piece of metal across the two terminals? "Are there any NEVER rules for dry cells?" I asked. "Only one," said Dad. "NEVER put a piece of metal across the terminals. If you do, you will cause a short circuit and burn out the dry cell. Take care of these little power stations."

Dad opened my flashlight and removed the small dry cells. He gave one to my sister and one to me.

In how many ways can we use dry cells? "This fine invention is very useful to many people. What a help it is for those who have to walk in places where lighting a match or candle would be dangerous!

"When the farmer has to attend to his livestock in the barn, a match or candle could be very dangerous."

"That's right," said Susan Jane. "One slip and the whole barn could be set on fire."

"What about the coal miner who has to go poking around in the dark?" I suggested. "There are gases there that could cause an explosion if he lit a match."

"You are both right," said Dad. "And don't forget how Doctor Ross uses his flashlight to look at your throats. He carries it in his pocket like a fountain pen. The dry cell is used now more than ever before."

"How does a dry cell work?" I asked.

WAX OR ASPHALT

CENTER OR
PLUS TERMINAL

ZINC CASE OR
MINUS TERMINAL

GRAPHITE
+
MANGANESE DIOXIDE
+
AMMONIUM CHLORIDE

CARBON
ROD

POROUS
CARDBOARD

DIAGRAM OF A DRY CELL

"If you were to look inside one, you would see chemicals. They are ready to work — quietly and efficiently — to serve you when you press a button or flip a switch. There are no secret words to say to make it work. Anyone can learn how to do it. It's easy and it's fun. In fact, you can teach it to your friends.

Can you name some of the parts of a dry cell?

"Just as a magnet has two poles, north and south, so a dry cell has two poles, plus and minus. Do you see the center rod? That's made of carbon — the plus side. The case around the cell is usually made of a metal called zinc. That is the minus pole."

Why is it called a dry cell?

Dad took his hacksaw and cut a dry cell down the center.

"Now we are coming to the chemical plant that manufactures the electrical energy we sometimes call electrons. It's made into a hard paste so that it can be carried about. That's one of the reasons these cells are called 'dry cells.'"

Why is a storage battery called a "battery" and not a "cell"?

"Does our car use the same kind of battery or dry cell?" I asked.

"It is a battery, but not a dry cell," answered Dad. "The car battery is called a storage battery. It does not use a hard paste like your flashlight cell. We may call it a wet battery."

"A wet battery?" Susan Jane echoed.

26

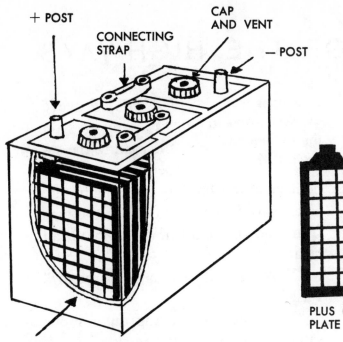

+ POST

CONNECTING STRAP

CAP AND VENT

— POST

CASE DIVIDED INTO 3 COMPARTMENTS OR CELLS

DIAGRAM OF A STORAGE BATTERY

STRAP TO CONNECT MINUS AND PLUS TERMINALS OF ADJOINING CELLS

SEVERAL OF THESE PLATES AND SEPARATORS IN EACH CELL

PLUS (POSITIVE) PLATE

RUBBER SEPARATOR

MINUS (NEGATIVE) PLATE

What are the two liquids used in a storage battery?

"Right. It uses distilled water and an acid — a very dangerous acid."

"Do you mean that our car battery also makes electrons like a chemical plant?" I asked.

"A chemical plant is correct," smiled Dad. "The storage battery in our car is a real power station. It starts our motor and helps it run. It makes our light go on. It wipes the windows in a rainstorm. It runs our heater in the winter. It gives our radio power. My cigarette lighter uses the battery. Even the windows open and close in my new car, thanks to the battery."

"Why do we use distilled water? Is it cleaner?" I wanted to know.

"Why do we need acid, if it's so dangerous?" asked Susan Jane.

Why does the storage battery use distilled water?

"Distilled water, like rain water, does not have any impurities," said Dad. "And the acid combines with the lead to give us electricity. The car uses the battery to spark the gasoline in the motor to get it started. Without it the car wouldn't move."

Dad motioned for us to come over to his car. He raised the hood and we peered in to see the battery. "The storage battery in the car is not as safe to touch as the dry cell in your flashlight, Mike. The acid can cause a severe burn and make holes in our clothing.

"Do you remember the NEVER game?" Dad asked us.

"We sure do," answered my sister.

"Good. NEVER touch any part of the battery when the motor is on."

Mother walked over to us. "How would you junior scientists like to climb into this chemical or electrical or gasoline-operated machine and take a ride with me? I'll need some help with the groceries," she said.

27

THE POLICEMAN OF THE HIGHWAYS

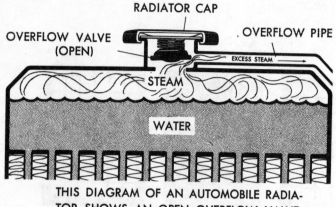

RADIATOR CAP

OVERFLOW VALVE (OPEN)

OVERFLOW PIPE

EXCESS STEAM

STEAM

WATER

THIS DIAGRAM OF AN AUTOMOBILE RADIATOR SHOWS AN OPEN OVERFLOW VALVE, ALLOWING EXCESS STEAM TO ESCAPE. SUCH A VALVE IS NEEDED IN ORDER TO RELIEVE STEAM PRESSURE.

How does the overflow valve in the automobile protect it?

THERE were many cars on the road to the supermarket, and a policeman was on duty directing traffic. Every so often he would stop the cars from moving until the traffic ahead cleared up.

"Why can't he let us go through?" I asked.

"The officer is looking out for our safety," Mother explained.

"He is like a safety valve," said Dad, "just as we have safety valves in locomotives and in the radiator of this car. These valves are seldom used, but they are very important. They are the policemen of these machines. When the locomotive has worked up too much steam and is in danger of exploding, the safety valve releases the extra steam. The same thing happens in the radiator of the car."

The policeman signaled us to go ahead.

ONE WAY

Why is the fuse often called the twenty-four-hour policeman?

"Just as the policeman stops traffic to make sure that the cars don't crash into one another, so a fuse in our home stops electrons from overcrowding. For when too many lines are plugged into one outlet, the electrons, like the cars, begin crashing into each other. When that happens, the extra movement makes the wires warm. The wires may get so hot that the walls of the house could catch fire.

"The fuse stops these electrons just as they begin to get hot. 'Stop,' says the policeman. 'Blow,' says the fuse. The lights go out. The toaster stops toasting and the broiler stops broiling."

"Too many electrical appliances were on at one time. They overloaded the circuit. That was one of the NEVER rules," I said.

"Very good, Mike. You learned quickly. It was a good thing that the fuse was there. Remember that the little fuse box is our policeman. It is guarding our home and our lives," said Dad. "Sometimes, instead of fuses, our houses have circuit breakers. These are safety devices, just like fuses. When too much current flows through the wires, the circuit breaker opens, which causes the electricity to stop flowing. Unlike fuses, circuit breakers can be reused."

A FUSE IS AN ELECTRICAL SAFETY DEVICE. WHEN TOO MUCH ELECTRIC CURRENT IS FLOWING, A PIECE OF METAL IN THE FUSE MELTS. THIS BREAKS THE CIRCUIT. WITHOUT A FUSE TO BREAK THE CIRCUIT, VERY STRONG CURRENT COULD CAUSE A FIRE.

ACTIVITIES FOR JUNIOR ELECTRICIANS

TRY these activities. Don't worry if you are not too successful at first. Follow the directions and diagrams as carefully as you can. You will have a great deal of fun.

Remember: When you see the word "wire" it means insulated wire. When it says, "connect wire," it means that the ends of the wire are to be stripped of insulation, material or paint.

NO. 1. HOW DOES YOUR FLASHLIGHT WORK?

You will use:
Flashlight
Piece of wire

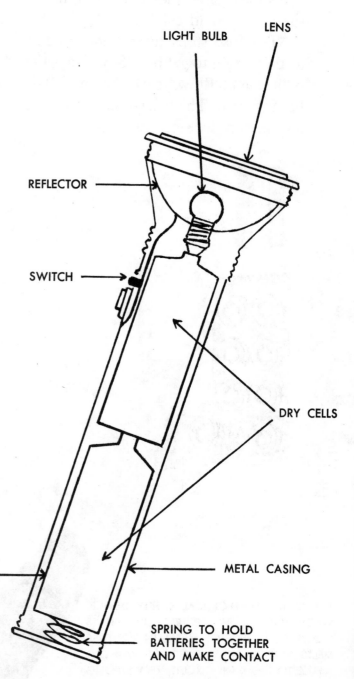

Do this:

Turn your flashlight on and then off. Now that you are sure the flashlight works, take it apart to see the different parts.

Strip the insulation from both ends of a piece of wire about six inches long.

Wrap one end of the bare wire around the base of the bulb that you removed from the flashlight.

Touch the bottom of the bulb to the center terminal of the cell.

Touch the end of the wire to the bottom of the cell.

The light goes on.

Why it works:

When you closed the switch of the flashlight, you completed a circuit. That is, you provided a closed path for the current to follow in a circle.

LIGHT BULB

LENS

REFLECTOR

SWITCH

DRY CELLS

ZINC CONTAINER

METAL CASING

SPRING TO HOLD BATTERIES TOGETHER AND MAKE CONTACT

You will use:
  Dry cell (large or small)
  Flashlight bulb
  Miniature socket
  Wire
  Piece of metal
  Block of wood
  Two nails
  Hammer

Do this:

Do you remember *Activity No. 1?* We were able to turn the light on by touching the wire to the cell.

Then we removed the wire and the light went out.

That's pretty simple. But an easier way is to use a switch.

Take a piece of metal — four inches long, and one inch wide. (You can cut it from a tin can if you are careful.)

Nail one end of it on the block of wood.

Place another nail in the wood under the other end of the metal.

Do not place either nail all the way down in the wood.

Be sure that the loose end of the metal is not resting on the nail beneath.

Now you have a switch.

Connect one wire from either terminal of the dry cell to the nail under the metal.

Remember to strip off the insulation from the ends of all the wires you use.

Connect a second wire from the other terminal of the dry cell to either terminal of the miniature socket.

Connect a third wire from the other terminal of the socket to the nail holding the strip of metal in place.

Now press the switch.

If you have made all the connections properly, the circuit is closed and the light will go on.

Save this switch. You will use it many times in these activities.

Why it works:

If you have a large dry cell, you will notice two terminals at the top. Connecting wires to them is done much more easily than with the small flashlight cell.

But all of these activities can be done with either cell, except that the large cell lasts longer and it is easier to use.

Each cell gives us 1½ volts.

Connect the wires the way you did in *Activity No. 1.*

The switch is a convenient way for us to open and close a circuit. It is easier than connecting and disconnecting wires. It is also a safer way to turn the lights and other electrical appliances on and off.

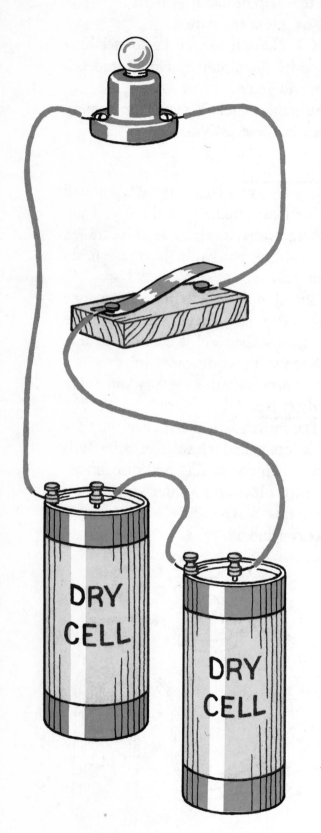

You will use:
  Two dry cells
  Wire
  Switch
  Flashlight bulb
  Miniature socket

<u>*Do this:*</u>

Do you remember how bright the bulb was in *Activity No. 2?* Now let's see what happens when we add another dry cell to the circuit. Of course, it has to be connected properly.

Connect one wire between the center terminal of cell 1 and the end terminal of cell 2.

The remainder of the connections are similar to the way you did them in the previous activity.

One wire is connected between the terminal of cell 1 and a socket terminal, and a second wire connects the other socket terminal to either nail on the switch.

The last wire connects the other nail with cell 2's center terminal.

Press the switch.

See how much brighter the light bulb is?

<u>*Why it works:*</u>

The two dry cells connected in series resulted in about twice the power of one cell.

This made the bulb brighter.

When you connected two cells of 1½ volts each in series, you really added them.

How many volts do you have now?

Would you like to try it with an electric bell?

NO. 4. HOW CAN WE CONNECT TWO DRY CELLS TO MAKE THEM LAST LONGER?

You will use:
    Two dry cells
    Wire
    Switch
    Flashlight bulb
    Miniature socket

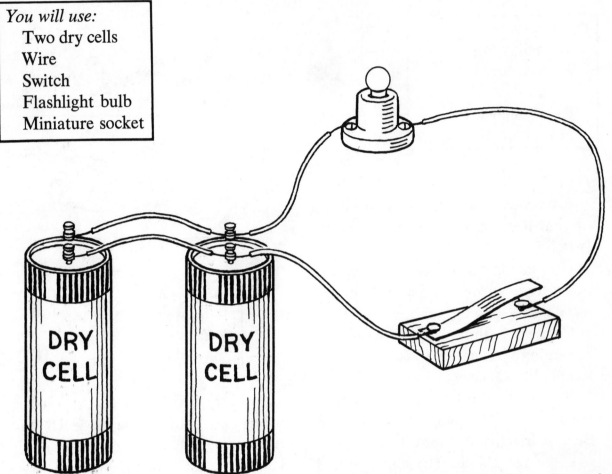

Do this:

Connect the dry cells, wires, switch and bulb as shown in the illustration.

First connect one dry cell in a circuit with your switch and the light bulb.

If you have forgotten how to do it, go back to *Activity No. 2.*

Now connect two other wires to the terminals on cell 2.

Take the wire from the center terminal of cell 2 and connect it to the center terminal of cell 1.

Take the wire coming from the end terminal of cell 2 and connect it to the end terminal of cell 1.

You should now have two wires connected to each of the terminals of cell 1.

Press the switch.

Notice that the light is not any brighter than it was when only one cell was in the circuit.

Why it works:

You connected the two dry cells in parallel.

No, the light is not brighter than it was with one dry cell.

That is why parallel connections are better when cells are to be used over a long period of time.

NO. 5. HOW CAN WE CONNECT SEVERAL LIGHT BULBS IN SERIES?

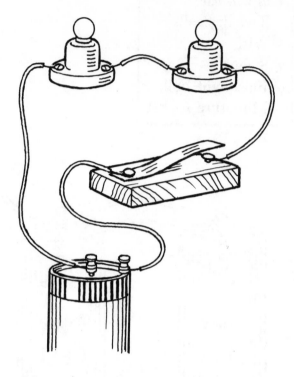

You will use:
- Dry cell
- Wire
- Switch
- Two flashlight bulbs
- Two miniature sockets

Do this:

Connect one wire from one terminal of your dry cell to one terminal of the switch.

Now connect a second wire from the other terminal of the dry cell to one terminal of socket 1.

Connect a third wire between the remaining terminal of socket 1 to one terminal of socket 2.

Now connect a fourth wire between the remaining terminal of socket 2 to the last terminal of the switch.

Close the switch. The bulbs should light.

Each bulb is not as bright as it was when we used one in our circuit.

Now unscrew one bulb. The other bulb will go out.

Why it works:

When both bulbs were lit, electricity was flowing in a complete path through the circuit. It was able to flow out of the dry cell right through the bulbs and return to the dry cell — like a merry-go-round.

This is called connecting bulbs in series.

In *Activity No. 2* we used one dry cell having 1½ volts to light one bulb. The little bulb was bright.

Now we divided that 1½ volts between two bulbs in series. Each bulb received only ¾ of a volt.

Do you see why the bulbs in series were a bit dim?

When you unscrewed one bulb, the other one went out.

Do you know why?

Because you interrupted the circuit. The electrons were not flowing in a merry-go-round.

Oh, yes, did you know that the tiny wire in the little bulb you removed was part of the path through which the electrons flow?

Our homes, stores and offices are all wired in parallel. If they were connected in series, all of the lights would be on and appliances running at one time or not at all. Wiring in parallel is surely more practical!

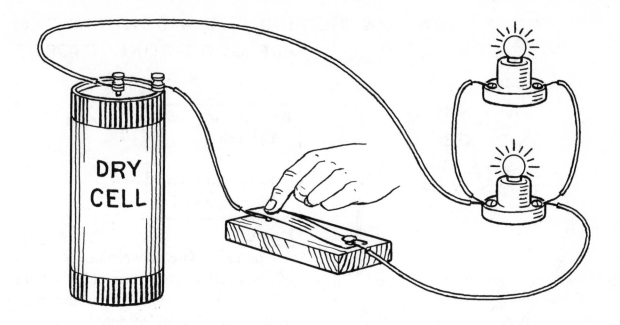

NO. 6. HOW CAN WE CONNECT SEVERAL LIGHT BULBS IN PARALLEL?

You will use:
Dry cell
Wire
Switch
Two flashlight bulbs
Two miniature sockets

Do this:

Connect your dry cell, switch and one socket in a complete circuit.

Press the switch. See how bright it is? Try to remember how it looks.

Now we are going to bring another bulb into our circuit.

In *Activity No. 5* we connected them in series.

Do you remember the disadvantages of that circuit?

Connect a wire between one terminal of socket 1, already in the circuit, to one terminal of socket 2.

Now connect another wire between the other terminals of sockets 1 and 2. Notice that there are two wires com-ing out of each terminal of socket 1.

Press the switch. Both bulbs should light.

Are you surprised to find that each bulb is just as bright as the single bulb you lit at the start of this activity?

Now unscrew one bulb. The other one remains lit.

More surprises!

Why it works:

You have connected two bulbs in parallel.

Each bulb has its own path to and from the dry cell.

The path does not have to go through both bulbs as it did in a series circuit.

Try tracing the path of the electric current to each bulb.

Since each bulb is connected directly to the dry cell, each is as bright as if you had only one bulb.

Now if one bulb goes out, the other remains lit, as in your own house.

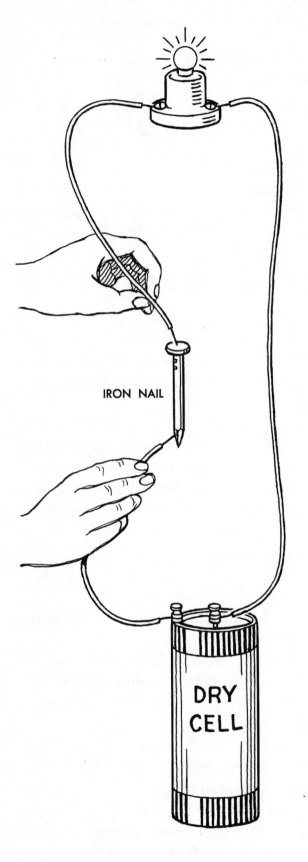

IRON NAIL

DRY CELL

You will use:
Dry cell
Wire
Flashlight bulb
Miniature socket

Do this:

Connect a wire between one terminal of a dry cell and one terminal of a light socket. Attach one end of another wire to the other dry cell terminal.

Attach a third wire to the other terminal of the socket.

The ends of the two wires should be free.

Touch the two free ends of the wire together briefly.

You have now completed the circuit and the light should go on.

Touch the two free ends of the wires to opposite ends of an iron nail. The light will go on.

Test other materials in this manner to see which ones help the light go on.

Why it works:

Until now we have used wires to complete our circuits. We saw how a nail acted in the same way.

As you see, some metals are good conductors of electricity. Some are better than others.

If you test glass, wood, plastic, or rubber, you will find that the light will not go on. Not enough electricity passes through them to light the bulb.

These materials are called non-conductors.

You will use:
Dry cell
Wire
Flashlight bulb
Miniature socket
Cardboard
Nail

Do this:

Use the nail to punch six holes down the left side of a piece of cardboard, and six holes down the right side.

Place the end of one wire in any hole at the left and the other end in any hole at the right.

Strip the insulation from the ends of the wire and secure it in place.

Repeat this with five other wires.

You now have six wires in place in a haphazard way.

Set this aside for a while.

Connect a wire between a dry cell terminal and a socket terminal.

Connect another wire to the remaining terminal of the dry cell.

Now attach a third wire to the remaining terminal of the socket.

This is similar to your conductor tester in *Activity No. 7.*

Touch the two free ends of the wires together briefly. The light will go on.

Hold the cardboard so that you cannot see how the wires are connected.

Place the name of a baseball player on the left side, which will serve as the question, and the name of his team on the right side, which will be the answer.

Be sure that the player and team are on opposite ends of the same wire.

Ask your friend to take the two free ends of the wires from the cell and socket. Now try to touch the matching questions and answers.

Why it works:

By touching the question with one end of the wire, and the answer with the other end of the wire, the light will go on. This happens because the circuit has been completed.

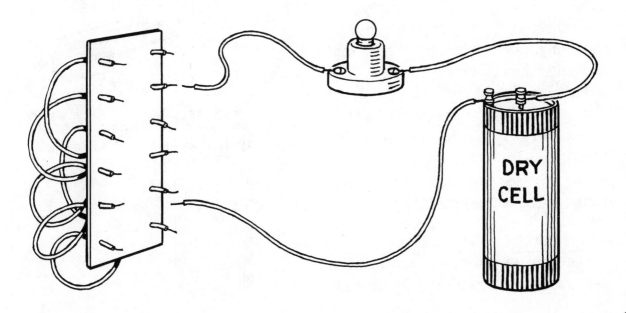

You will use:
  Dry cell
  Wire
  Flashlight bulb
  Miniature socket
  Tin foil
  Block of wood
  Two thumbtacks

Do this:

Cut a piece of tin foil so that the center is as thin as a piece of wire.

Secure it to a block of wood with two thumbtacks. Do not push the tacks all the way down. Set this aside for a while.

Strip about two inches of insulation away from the middle portion of two wires. Connect these wires to the two terminals of a miniature socket.

Connect the other end of one of these wires to a dry cell terminal.

Connect the other end of the second wire to one of the thumbtacks of your fuse board.

Be sure that the stripped end of the wire is in contact with the metal of the tack.

Connect a third wire between the remaining dry cell terminal and the remaining thumbtack.

The light should go on.

Lay a bare wire or any piece of metal across the two bare wires. The light will go out.

Did you see how the tin-foil fuse melted at the narrow part?

Why it works:

The light went on because the circuit was complete. Electricity flowed through the tin-foil fuse, as it does in our homes.

When you placed a piece of metal across the two bared wires, you caused a short circuit. Electricity was able to flow back to the dry cell without passing through the bulb to light it.

The electricity that was not used by the bulb caused the wires to become hotter. The tin-foil strip melts at a lower temperature than the other wires. When this happened, the circuit was broken and no more electricity flowed.

The fuse protects us by burning out. If the fuse were not there, the wires would have become hotter and hotter. This could have resulted in a fire.

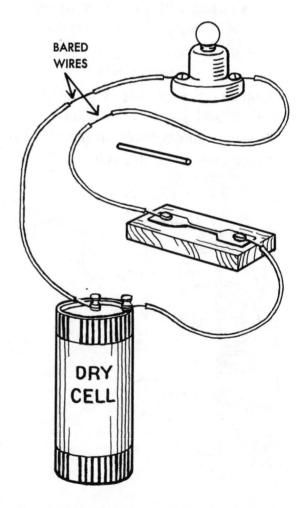

BARED
WIRES

DRY
CELL

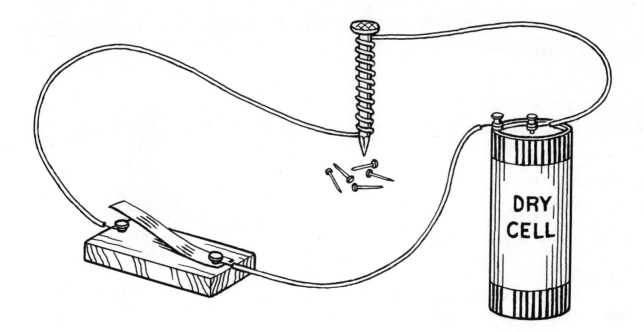

NO. 10. HOW CAN WE MAKE AN ELECTROMAGNET?

You will use:
- Dry cell
- Wire
- Switch
- Large nail
- Small nails or paper clips

Do this:

Wind about ten turns of wire around a large nail.

Strip the insulation from the ends of the wire.

Connect one end of the wire to one terminal of a dry cell and the other end to the terminal of the switch.

Prepare a second wire. Connect this wire to the other terminal of the dry cell and the other end to the switch.

Now close the switch and try to pick up paper clips or small nails with the large nail.

Open the switch and the small nails, or the paper clips, will fall down.

Why it works:

The electricity from one part of the dry cell flows through the many turns of wire back into the dry cell.

When electricity flows through a wire, the wire has magnetic power around it. If the wire happens to be in the form of a coil, the magnetism is even stronger.

Now, when we put an iron nail inside the coil, the nail becomes a magnet. This is true only for as long as the electricity is flowing in the circuit. It is a magnet when you want it to be.

Do you see how magnets and electricity are related?

Our magnet really depends on the electricity it gets from the dry cell.

We find electromagnets all around us.

We find them in refrigerators, in television sets, telephones, in Dad's electric shaver and in Mother's vacuum cleaner.

NO. 11. HOW CAN WE MAKE AN ELECTROMAGNET STRONGER?

You will use:
Dry cell
Wire
Switch
Large nail
Small nails

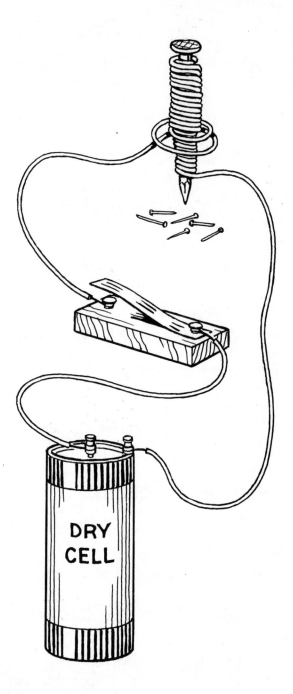

DRY CELL

Do this:

Connect your electromagnet in the same way that you did in *Activity No. 10* — except for one thing. This time wind *twenty-five* turns of wire around the large nail.

Close the switch. See how many small nails you can pick up.

Do this two more times.

Do you know how to find the average number of nails picked up?

Add the number of nails picked up in three tries. Then divide by three.

This will give you the average number of nails picked up by the electromagnet with the twenty-five turns of wire.

Write the average down.

Now that you are an expert, wrap twenty-five more turns of wire around the nail, making fifty turns all together.

Count the number of nails you can pick up this time. Do this two more times.

Find the average number of nails picked up by your electromagnet with fifty turns of wire. Write this down.

Compare the two averages. You will see that more nails were picked up by the electromagnet with more turns.

Why it works:

The more turns of wire you have, the more magnetism there is around the coil, and the stronger the electromagnet.

You may have found that you picked up about twice as many nails when you doubled the number of turns.

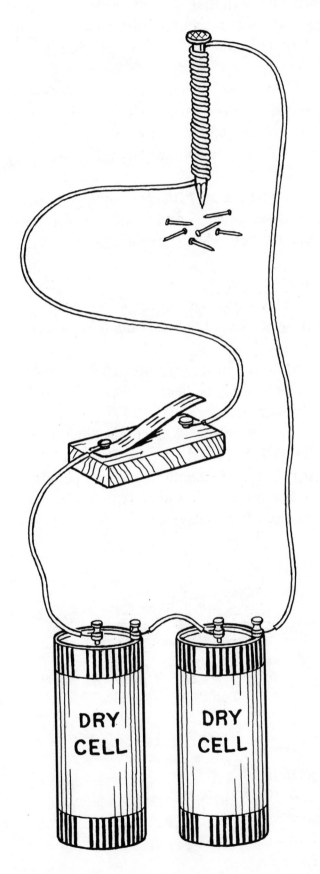

You will use:
Two dry cells
Wire
Switch
Large nail
Small nails

Do this:

Do you remember how to connect two dry cells in series to give us more electricity?

You must remember to connect one wire between the plus or center terminal of one dry cell to the minus or end terminal of the other cell.

Connect a second wire from the other terminal of one cell to one terminal of the switch.

Wrap twenty-five turns of wire around a large nail.

Connect one end of the electromagnet to the free terminal of the cell and the other end to the switch.

Close the switch and see how many nails you can pick up. Try it three times to find an average number.

How does it compare with the number picked up previously?

Why it works:

When we connect two dry cells in series, we get twice as much electricity than we do with one cell. That is, we get 3 instead of 1½ volts from one cell.

Then we can be sure that if we want a stronger magnet, we must send more electricity through the coils.

You will use:
Dry cell
Wire
Switch
Two nails
Screw
Piece of metal
Block of wood

Do this:

Bend the piece of metal into the Z-shape shown in the diagram.

Nail it on the block of wood.

Hammer two nails into the wood so that they are just under the free end of the metal strip.

Connect a fairly long length of wire to one terminal of a dry cell.

Wind the wire several times around one of the nails, beginning at the top and working down.

Then bring the wire across to the other nail and wind it around as many times as the other one, working upward.

Connect the other end of this wire to one terminal of your switch.

Connect a second wire between the free terminal of the dry cell and the switch.

Close the switch. The sounder — the Z-shaped metal — will be attracted to the two nails underneath it.

You may have to adjust the sounder before it will work.

You have now made a simple telegraph sounder — and found a practical use for your electromagnet.

Why it works:

Electricity flowing through the coils of wire around the nails made the nails magnetic.

The sounder was attracted to the nails as long as electricity was flowing through the circuit.

The famous American inventor Samuel F. B. Morse, in 1844, made it possible to communicate with people in distant places by signals through the means of the telegraph.

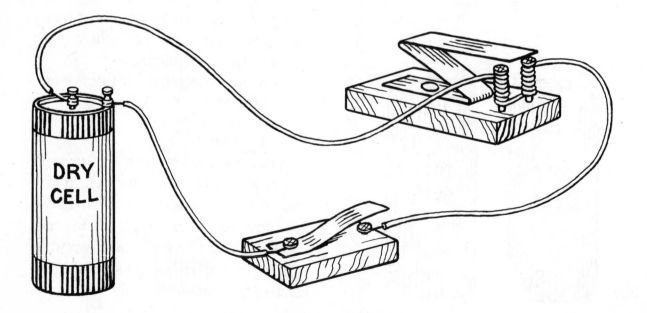

NO. 14. HOW CAN WE MAKE AN ELECTRIC CURRENT DETECTOR?

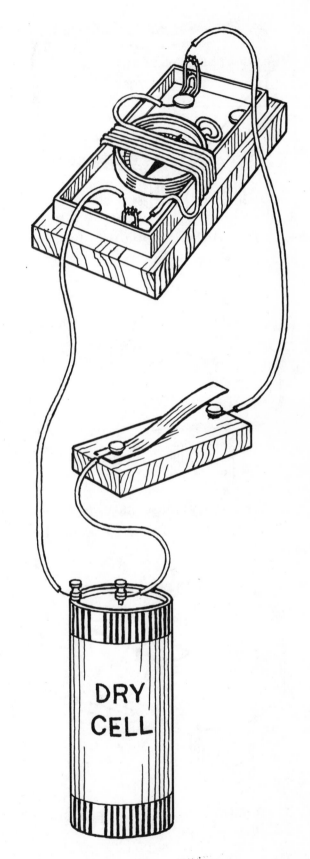

You will use:
- Dry cell
- Long wire
- Magnetic compass
- Block of wood
- Cover of small cardboard box
- Four thumbtacks
- Two paper clips

Do this:

Wrap about ten turns of insulated wire around the cover of a box.

Strip the insulation from the ends of the wire.

Place the box on a block of wood and secure it in place with some thumbtacks.

Bend two paper clips in half, as shown.

Wrap the ends of the wires around the thumbtacks. Slip the paper clips under the tacks before pressing them into the wood.

The paper clips will be your leads.

Place your magnetic compass inside the box.

Connect a wire between a dry cell terminal and a switch terminal.

Connect two other wires from the cell and switch to the paper clip leads.

Close the switch. The compass needle will move.

Open and close the switch several times.

Why it works:

Do you remember that when electricity moves through a coil, magnetism is all around it? That magnetism goes right through the glass to the magnetic needle and moves it.

43

Some of the important ideas presented in this book are summarized below. As you read them, you may want to go back and refresh your memory.

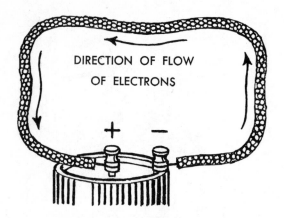

1. Electricity is made up of moving electrons.

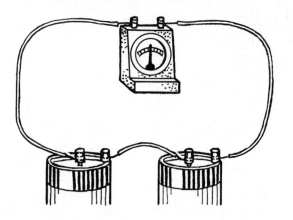

4. More than one cell connected in series will give more power than a single cell.

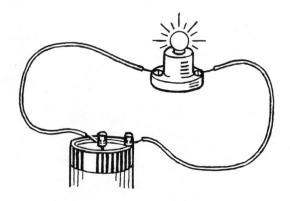

2. Electricity must have a complete circuit if it is to be used.

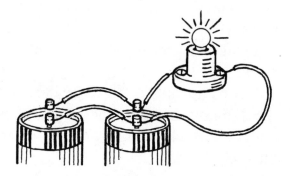

5. More than one cell connected in parallel will give longer life than a single cell.

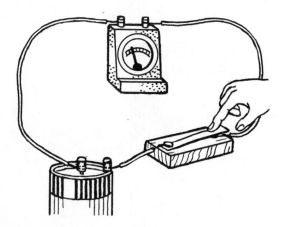

3. A switch is used to open and close circuits.

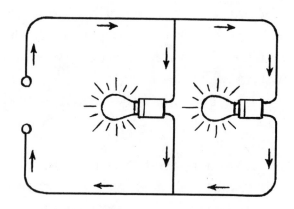

6. Lights in our homes are wired in parallel.

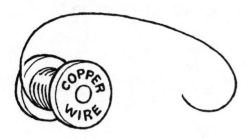

7. Some materials, particularly metals, carry electricity better than others. These materials are called good conductors.

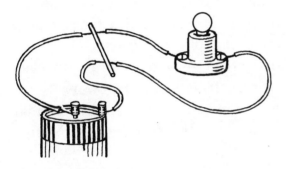

8. A short circuit occurs when the current can flow through an easy short cut instead of going through the regular circuit.

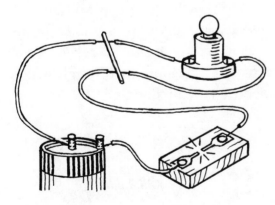

9. A fuse protects us from damage due to short circuits, or from using too much electricity at the same time.

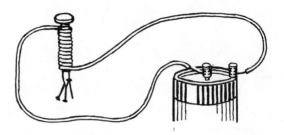

10. Electricity flowing through a coil of wire around an iron core, makes the core into a magnet for as long as electricity is flowing. This is an electromagnet.

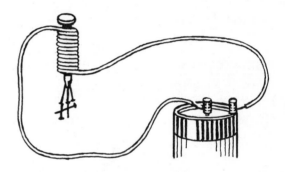

11. The strength of an electromagnet can be increased by increasing the number of coil turns.

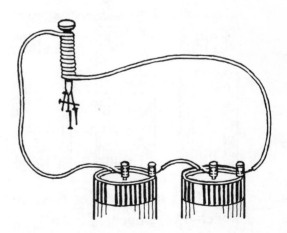

12. The strength of an electromagnet can also be increased by adding dry cells to the circuit.

SOME IMPORTANT TERMS
FOR YOU TO REMEMBER

Alternating current: An electric current whose direction of flow is changed at periodic intervals (many times per second).

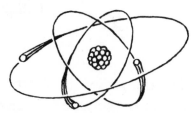

Ammeter: An instrument for measuring the strength of an electric current.

Ampere: A unit that measures the rate of flow of electric current.

Atom: The tiniest part of an element.

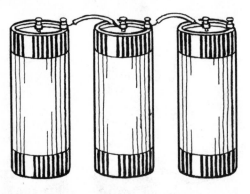

Battery: Two or more electrical cells connected together.

Circuit: Entire path along which electricity can flow from the source through wires and appliances and back to the source.

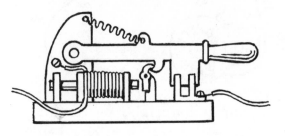

Circuit breaker: An automatic switch which breaks the circuit when too much electricity is flowing. It is similar to a fuse, but it can be reused.

Compound: A substance formed by a combination of elements.

Conductor: A good carrier of electricity. It acts as a highway.

Direct current: An electric current that flows in only one direction through a circuit.

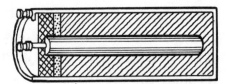

Dry cell: A self-contained voltaic cell whose electrolyte is a moist paste packed tightly around a carbon rod.

Electrolyte: A solution through which electricity can flow.

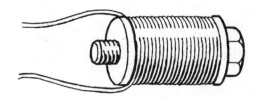

Electromagnet: A coil of wire wound around an iron core which becomes a magnet as long as electricity flows through the coil.

Electron: A negative or minus charge of electricity, the smallest now known.

Element: A substance made up of only one kind of atom.

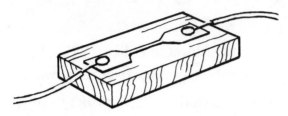

Fuse: A device which acts as a policeman to warn us of danger. The fuse melts when too many electrons are flowing. This breaks the circuit.

Galvanometer: An instrument for detecting direct currents of electricity.

Generator: A machine or dynamo that produces electricity from mechanical energy.

Horsepower: A unit for measuring power.

Insulator: A very poor conductor of electricity.

Kilowatt: One thousand watts.

Molecule: The tiniest part of a compound.

Ohm: A unit of measurement to gauge the resistance to the passage of electric current.

Ohmmeter: An instrument that measures electrical resistance.

Power: The rate of doing work.

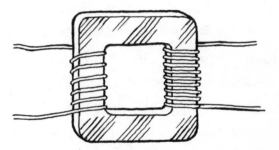

Transformer: A machine which can increase or decrease the voltage of an alternating current.

Volt: A unit that measures electrical pressure.

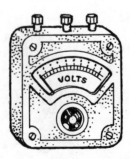

Voltmeter: A device for measuring voltage.

Watt: A unit for measuring electrical power.

47

SOME FAMOUS SCIENTISTS WHO MADE THE ELECTRICAL AGE POSSIBLE

Alessandro Volta (1745-1827), Italy, made the first cell that produced an electric current.

André Marie Ampère (1775-1836), France, developed the science of electromagnetism.

Georg Simon Ohm (1787-1854), Germany, worked with current electricity.

Michael Faraday (1791-1867), England, made the first electric generator.

James Watt (1736-1819), Scotland, invented the steam engine.

Samuel F. B. Morse (1791-1872), United States, invented the telegraph.

Alexander Graham Bell (1847-1922), United States, invented the telephone.

Guglielmo Marconi (1874-1937), Italy, first to send a message over radio waves.

Luigi Galvani (1737-1798), Italy, discovered that electricity is possible by chemical action.

Thomas Alva Edison (1847-1931), United States, invented the electric light bulb.

Hans Christian Oersted (1777-1851), Denmark, found that electricity and magnetism are related.

Charles Proteus Steinmetz (1865-1923), United States, made many contributions in the field of electrical engineering.

VOLTA

FARADAY

AMPERE

BELL

THE HOW AND WHY WONDER BOOK OF
MACHINES

By DR. JEROME J. NOTKIN, Science Supervisor, Suffolk County, N. Y.
  Professor, Hofstra College
  and SIDNEY GULKIN, M. S. in Ed., Teacher, New York City
Illustrated by GEORGE J. ZAFFO
Editorial Production: DONALD D. WOLF

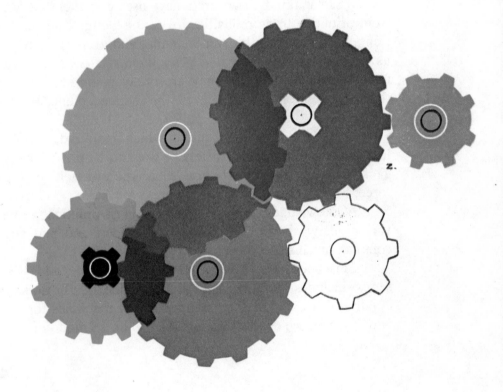

Edited under the supervision of
  Dr. Paul E. Blackwood,
  Washington, D. C.

Text and illustrations approved by
  Oakes A. White, Brooklyn Children's Museum, Brooklyn, New York

GROSSET & DUNLAP • Publishers • NEW YORK

Introduction

The people of very early times may have used machines in primitive ways. As mankind discovered new uses for them, it was able to move from primitive to more civilized ways of living. And the history of civilization almost parallels the ever-widening and ever-wiser use of machines. But, as we learn in this *How and Why Wonder Book,* no matter how complex today's machines appear, they are really combinations of two or more of the six simple ones — the lever, the inclined plane, the wedge, the screw, the wheel and axle, and the pulley.

It is these simple machines which mankind, through the ages, has learned to use in a great variety of ways to help it do its work more easily. This book describes clearly how each type of machine is useful in applying force, in order to make work easier.

A knowledge of simple machines is of practical value to us as we do various daily chores. It also helps us understand and appreciate how the complex machines do their work.

This book, like several others in the *How and Why Wonder Book* series, includes several interesting experiments. By doing the experiments, children will discover some of the laws of machines for themselves and see why it is that we depend on machines to do so much of the world's work.

Paul E. Blackwood

Dr. Blackwood is a professional employee in the U. S. Office of Education. This book was edited by him in his private capacity and no official support or endorsement by the Office of Education is intended or should be inferred.

Library of Congress Catalog Card Number: 60-51559

1983 PRINTING

Contents

Page

THE MACHINE AGE 4
BREAKING THROUGH THE
    LANGUAGE BARRIER 4
  What is work? 4
  How is work measured? 5
  What is power? 6
  What is efficiency? 6
  Why is work hard? 6
  What is energy? 7
  How does energy become active? 7
  Machines 8
  What is a machine? 8
  Why are machines used? 8
  Was there ever a time without machines? 8
  What are the six basic machines? 9
THE LEVER 10
  How does the lever make work easier? . . 10
  What is the "Law of the Lever"? 12
  What are the three classes of levers? . . . 12
  Why are scissors a double lever? 13
  What is a second-class lever? 13
  What is a third-class lever? 14
  How You Can Experiment With a Lever 15
THE INCLINED PLANE 16
  How does the inclined plane help in
    building? 16
  How does the inclined plane make work
    easier? 17
  How do you figure out the law of the
    inclined plane? 19
  *How You Can Experiment With an
    Inclined Plane* 20
THE WEDGE 20
  How is the wedge related to the inclined
    plane? 20
  How is the wedge used? 21
  What is the advantage of using the
    wedge? 21
THE SCREW 21
  How is the screw related to the inclined
    plane? 21

Page

  What is the pitch? 22
  *How You Can Make a Screw Out of an
    Inclined Plane* 23
  Why We Use Screws 23
THE WHEEL 24
  Why was the invention of the wheel
    important? 24
  What do we know about the develop-
    ment of the wheel? 24
  What makes the wheel a basic machine? 25
  How can wheels turn other wheels? 27
  Why is a meat grinder handle longer
    than that of a pencil sharpener? 28
  How You Can Experiment With a Wheel 28
  How can you reduce friction? 28
  How to Make a Lift Truck 30
  How to Make a Freight Elevator 32
THE PULLEY 33
  Why is the pulley often called a wheel
    with ropes? 33
  How does the single fixed pulley work? . 34
  How is the movable pulley used? 35
  How does the combination of pulleys
    work? 36
  How strong are you? 37
  How You Can Experiment With Pulleys 37
  Where does the word "pulley" come
    from? 39
THE SOURCES OF ENERGY 40
  What are the different kinds of energy? 41
HOW MAN HARNESSED THE
    FORCES OF NATURE 42
  How has man harnessed the forces of
    Nature? 42
  *How You Can Make a Model Water
    Wheel* 44
  What are some other sources of energy? 44
  What is an engine? 44
SOME IMPORTANT IDEAS FOR YOU
    TO REMEMBER 45
SOME IMPORTANT TERMS FOR YOU
    TO REMEMBER 46

The Machine Age

The word "machine" comes from a Greek word, *mechos,* meaning "expedient" or something that makes easy. The Romans used the Latin word *machina,* a word which meant "trick" or "device." The Hebrew word for "machine" is *mechonah,* and as used in the Old Testament and in other Hebrew writings, was variously interpreted as "foundation," "base," "plan." In an age, long ago, when people had to do all kinds of work by hand, it is not surprising that they searched for "expedients" or "tricks" or "plans" to make their work easier. And they found them. Today, so many jobs are done by machine that the age in which we live is often called the Machine Age.

Breaking Through the Language Barrier

A while ago we saw a clown in the circus struggling to lift a chair which had been nailed to the floor by another clown. We could tell how great an effort our clown was making because he got red in the face and started to perspire. No matter how hard he tried, however, the chair wouldn't budge.

Did this clown do work?

Then another clown came out, picked up a feather from the chair and threw it into the air.

Did the second clown do work?

If your answer to the first question is

What is work?

yes and to the second one *no,* you are wrong both times.

Work, as spoken of in this book, occurs only when a *push* or a *pull* moves something with *weight* through a *distance.* The push or pull is called FORCE, and the weight is called RESISTANCE. Remember these two words well. We will need them throughout the entire book.

Going back to our clowns — the first clown tried to apply FORCE

(push or pull) to move the weight (the chair), but he did not move it. The second clown applied FORCE (push) and moved the RESISTANCE (the feather, which, however light, has weight) through a distance, by throwing it into the air.

When you have finished your home-

How is work measured? work, you may say that you have done "a lot." In science, we have to be more precise. We can't say: "The machine worked a lot." But we can say: "There was one *foot-pound* of work done." It sounds strange, but it is just another unit of measure. As the foot is a measure of distance, the foot-pound is a measure of an amount of work. We arrive at this measure by multiplying the force by the distance through which it acts.

Ten pounds raised four feet equals forty foot-pounds.

One foot-pound is the work done by a force of one pound acting through a distance of one foot.

If you lift a weight of ten pounds to a height of four feet, you do $10 \times 4 = 40$ foot-pounds of work, no matter how long it takes.

Which clown is doing work? Answer: The one on the right, because he is applying force and has moved the resistance (the feather).

Power is the rate of doing work. It is **What is power?** calculated by dividing the amount of work done by the time required to do it. The unit usually used to express this is *horsepower*. It is enough for now to know that a machine has one horsepower if its rate of work accomplishes 550 foot-pounds in one second (or 33,000 foot-pounds per minute).

Has someone ever told you that you **What is efficiency?** were not efficient in school? In practically the same way, we speak of efficiency of machines.

The efficiency of a machine is the *ratio* (comparative amount) of useful work it does to the total work input.

Inertia must be overcome before the car rolls and in order to accomplish work.

OUTPUT

INPUT

This picture study will help you understand *efficiency*.

$$\text{Efficiency} = \frac{\text{Work output}}{\text{Work input}}$$

Because of losses due to *friction* — that is, some form of rubbing action — no machine is able to deliver the same amount of work that is put into it.

You may know from having seen others **Why is work hard?** try to push a stalled automobile that it is more difficult to get it rolling than to push it after it has started to roll. This is due to the tendency of all bodies at rest to remain at rest. The scientists call this tendency *inertia*. You have to overcome the same inertia to stop a rolling automobile, because a body in motion tends to stay in motion. Thus, you have to overcome inertia to accomplish work.

Ask your friends whether it is easier to lift a pound of feathers or a pound of iron. They might answer wrongly that it is easier to lift the feathers. Measured in terms of work, it is the same. In both cases you lift a weight of one pound. But it is harder to lift two pounds than one pound, because you have to work harder to overcome the weight or the attraction of gravity.

Let's go back to pushing the automobile. If the owner has left the brakes set, it may be impossible to move the

There are many forms of energy — heat, electrical, mechanical and others.

How does energy become active? When energy is used in work, force is applied. This means that force is used to push or pull, to cause a body at rest to move, or to stop a moving body, or make it change its direction, or to cause a moving body to lose or gain speed.

car, and if he has left them partly set, it is much more difficult than with no brakes at all. This is due to the rubbing of the brakes against the wheels, or, as the scientists call it, *friction*. Thus, work is hard because matter has inertia and weight, and while working, we have to overcome friction.

What is energy? Perhaps at some time or other you were told: "Why don't you do something? You have much too much energy." Well, that's exactly what energy is: the ability or capacity to do something, to work.

Lift either weight. It's the same amount of work.

Overcoming friction helps the boy (right) to skate.

7

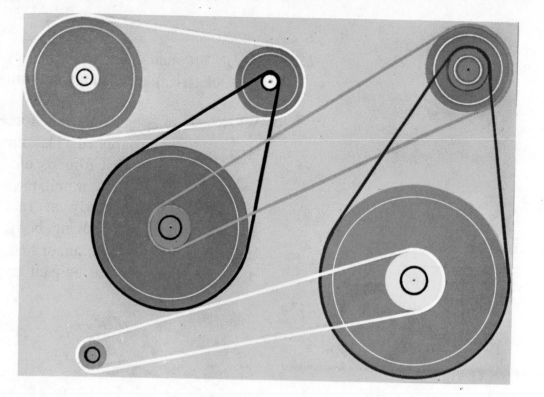

Machines

A man once spent considerable time constructing a contrivance made up of numerous gears, axles, levers, wheels and connecting belts. When all the moving parts were counted, the total reached about a thousand. It certainly looked quite impressive. But when the inventor was asked what this complicated device was supposed to do, his answer was: "Nothing at all!"

Was this really a machine? Not in the

What is a machine? true sense of the word. A machine, as we define it here, is a tool or device which, by applying a force (1) makes work easier, or (2) changes the direction of the force, or (3) increases the speed with which work is done. The device with a thousand moving parts, therefore, is not truly a machine, because it is not used to do any work at all.

In other words, we use machines be-

Why are machines used? cause they make possible a gain in *force*—that is, they enable us to overcome a great resistance with a small effort. When this is the case, we say that the machine gives us a *mechanical advantage* of force. Other machines enable us to move the resistance faster than the applied force is used. Such a machine gives us a *mechanical advantage of speed*.

Later on, as we discuss particular machines, we will figure out exactly how big these advantages are.

Living in a time that is called "The

Was there ever a time without machines? Machine Age," it is difficult to imagine that we did not always have the automobile, the airplane, the locomotive and all the other devices man has invented to make his work easier. But there was a time, thousands of years ago, when man had no machines at all, and until not too long ago he relied on the strength of his muscles or the muscles of animals for the energy necessary to operate the simple machines he had devised and constructed.

Even in very early times, man tried to use tools to make his work easier. These tools or machines were primitive, and were constructed because of need. In fact, these primitive machines are still used today in one form or another, and even our most complicated modern machines are combinations of the six basic ones already in use early in man's existence. The six basic machines are:

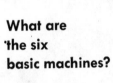

What are the six basic machines?

The wedge

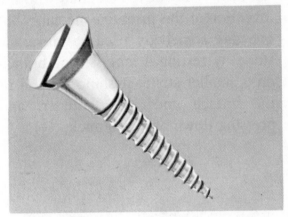

The screw

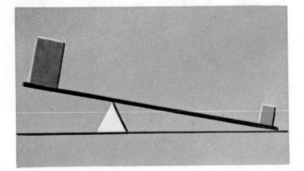

The lever

The wheel and axle

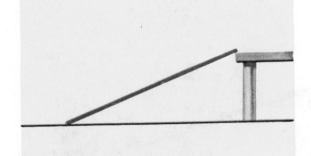

The slope, or inclined plane

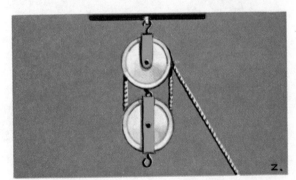

The pulley

9

The Lever

How does the lever make work easier?

Can you imagine primitive man trying to protect the entrance to his cave by putting a large boulder in front of it? He is a strong man, but not strong enough to lift the rock — not even strong enough to roll it. Nobody knows who first had the idea — nobody is credited with the invention of this primitive machine, but one day somebody tried to move the stone by resting a long, strong branch on a smaller stone, pushing the end of the branch under the boulder, and pressing down on the branch.

First-class Lever

Can you imagine the pride that man must have felt when he succeeded, without even too much effort, in moving the rock? He did not know that he had invented the machine which we call the "simple lever." By experience, primitive man found that the longer the lever, the more weight could be lifted with less effort. He learned this in the same way you found out where you have to sit on a seesaw to stay in balance, or that the farther you move from the point where a seesaw hinges on its rest,

the easier it is to lift your heavier playmate on the other end. The seesaw, too, is a lever.

The smaller stone in the first picture and the middle point of the seesaw have the same function: to provide a rest for the lever. This rest is called the *fulcrum*. The side where you apply the force is called the *effort*. The opposing side is called the *resistance*.

The lever need not always be straight, like the cave man's branch or the board of the seesaw. Sometimes the lever is

11

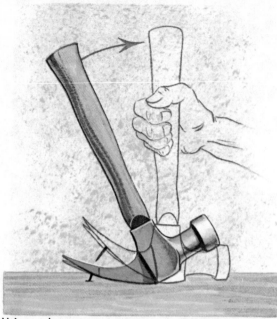

Using a hammer to remove a nail is using a lever.

Early man used the lever, as we have seen, but it was not until

What is the "Law of the Lever"? thousands of years later —about 240 B.C.—that the Greek scientist, Archimedes, discovered what we call the Law of the Lever: Two loads, A and B, balance when the scale-pan weight of A multiplied by its distance from the fulcrum is the same as the scale-pan weight of B multiplied by *its* distance from the fulcrum. As the force exerted on a machine is called effort, we call the distance from the effort to the fulcrum the *effort arm,* and the distance from the resistance to the fulcrum the *resistance arm.*

curved. When you pull a nail with a claw hammer, you are using a curved lever. The fulcrum is at the head of the hammer. You push down on the handle and the nail comes out. So, you see, we started with a primitive machine and find that it is still in use, in practically its original form, on the playground, in the house, and as part of more complicated machines.

There are three classes of levers, depending on the relative

What are the three classes of levers? position of the effort (E), fulcrum (F), and resistance (R). The first-class lever has F between E and R. Examples of the first-class lever are the crowbar, the seesaw and the pump handle. Now that you know Archimedes'

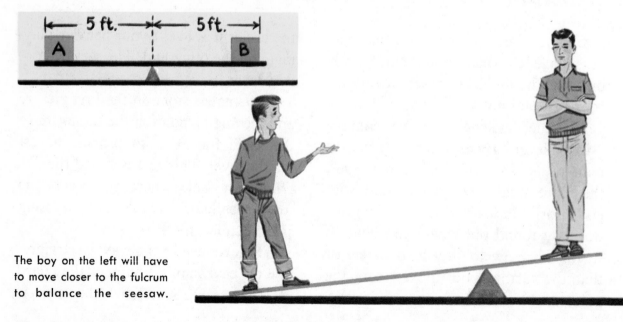

The boy on the left will have to move closer to the fulcrum to balance the seesaw.

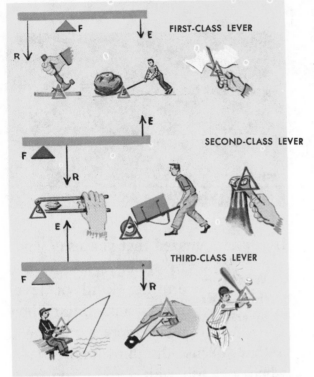

First-class lever: The fulcrum (F) is between the effort (E) and the resistance (R).

Second-class lever: The resistance (R) is between the fulcrum (F) and the effort (E).

Third-class lever: The effort (E) is between the fulcrum (F) and the resistance (R).

Law of the Lever, you can surprise your friends, after you know their weight, by figuring out exactly where you have to sit on the seesaw to balance your heavier or lighter companions — or, better still, where you have to put the lever on the fulcrum to be able to lift them up.

Why are scissors a double lever? Sometimes two levers are used together to form a double lever. A pair of scissors is such a double lever. The screw joining the two blades is the fulcrum. Try to cut a piece of cardboard with a regular pair of scissors and demonstrate for yourself the Law of the Lever. You will find that if you try to cut with the points of the scissors, you will not succeed. But when you use the scissors so that you cut close to the fulcrum, you will succeed because you have more force.

What is a second-class lever? We have seen that by using the long end of a lever we get more power and are able to do a hard job using little force. Look at the oars of a rowboat. The ends of the oars are the effort, the oarlocks are the resistance, and the pivotal points of the oars (the ends in the water) are the fulcrum.

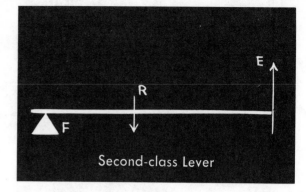

Second-class Lever

Watch closely when you row: The end of the oar in your hand — the effort end — moves farther than the resistance part in the oarlock. There is more force at the resistance. Just as in the case of the seesaw, we move the effort through a greater distance to get, in return, a greater force. So, in both cases, we trade distance or speed for more force. Other common examples of the second-class lever are the nutcracker and the wheelbarrow.

If you are amazed that you use a lever by riding a seesaw and another kind of lever rowing a boat, think how much more surprising it is that you use the third kind of lever when you fish with a rod. Stop for a moment and try to figure it out for yourself. Does it help if we tell you that in the third-class lever, the effort is between the fulcrum and the resistance? E is between F and R. The end of the

What is a third-class lever?

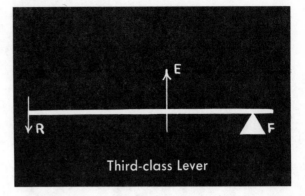

Third-class Lever

fishing pole nearest you is the fulcrum. The effort is the part you are holding and the resistance is at the far end of the pole. Here, for the first time, we exert more force at the effort than there is at the resistance. When you pull a fish out of the water, you will notice that the distance the resistance moves is greater than the distance the effort moves. Sugar tongs, our arms and legs, a broom and a baseball bat are other examples of this type of lever. In the third-class lever, we trade force for more distance and speed.

How You Can Experiment With a Lever

It is fun to check the Law of the Lever with a simple experiment. Build yourself a first-class lever with a ruler, a triangular piece of wood and two stones — a large one and a small one. Now try to figure out the following problems:

(1) where to put the ruler on the fulcrum to balance the two uneven weights.

(2) where to put the ruler to lift the heavier weight.

(3) whether it is possible to shift the ruler along the fulcrum until the weight of the ruler by itself lifts the weight.

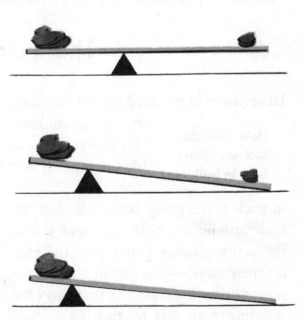

The ancient Egyptians used the principle of the inclined plane when they built pyramids about 4,000 years ago.

The Inclined Plane

Have you ever watched the construction of a large building? Have you wondered how so few men do the big job in such a relatively short time? If so, look around the next time and notice the many machines that help the men do their work — the steam shovel, the power drills, the elevators that carry the building materials to the floors high above the ground, as well as other equipment. Now think of the huge buildings of the ancient Romans, the Greeks, and — even earlier — the Egyptians. You surely have seen pictures of the pyramids, the tombs of the pharaohs and their queens. Just imagine these massive structures being built without the help of elevators and steam shovels—with only human effort as the source of power.

How does the inclined plane help in building?

16

Fewer men, less time and more machines are used to build skyscrapers than it took to build the pyramids.

A scientist once figured out that the Great Pyramid, built about 2885 B.C., contains 2,300,000 blocks of limestone, each weighing about two and a half tons. Is it surprising to learn that it took about 100,000 men twenty years to build? How did they manage to get the heavy blocks up to the necessary height? The lever was not much help in solving this problem. They did not have elevators, but they did have the slope, or inclined plane, another of the six simple machines. The inclined plane did not make it possible for them to do the work as fast as our modern machines, but it did make the project possible.

How does the inclined plane make work easier? Have you noticed that the long way up a hill is the easier way? It is also easier, as you will have noticed, to go up many shallow stairs leading to the same height. The ancient Egyptians had noticed these things, too, and they built a slope and pulled the stones into place instead of trying to carry them up. They did, on a large scale, the same thing a trucker does today when a barrel is too heavy for him to lift. He takes a flat surface — a heavy board, for example — places one end on the ground and the other end on the floor of the truck. Then he rolls the barrel onto the truck. That is exactly what an inclined plane is: a flat surface with one end higher than the other. A ramp is an inclined plane, and so is a mountain road. The inclined plane is used to help raise a body that is too heavy to be lifted straight up. Just as with the lever, this is accomplished by exerting a smaller force through a greater distance. The

The stairway leading to the front door of the house on the left is longer than the straight ladder shown in the back of the house. Still, it takes less effort to climb the stairway. The winding road (right) is an inclined plane.

amount of work is the same, whether the inclined plane is long or short, but it is easier to move the load over the longer distance. The less the angle of the inclined plane, the longer the distance and the less the effort needed.

Just as in the case of the lever, resistance times distance equals effort times distance. Now let's do some figuring: Suppose you want to lift fifty pounds five feet above the ground and you have a board ten feet long to make your inclined plane. Since the height above the ground is one-half

How do you figure out the law of the inclined plane?

of the length of the board, you would need only one-half of the weight of the force to pull the weight. In other words, twenty-five pounds of force should lift fifty pounds. Our arithmetic is right, but what about friction, which is the resistance caused when one object moves against another? We are safe in saying that in the example above, it takes a little more than twenty-five pounds to lift fifty pounds, and the smoother the board and the object to be moved, the less the resistance. If the object has wheels, the resistance is even less. That is why moving men usually put heavy furniture on a dolly before putting it on the ramp or other inclined plane.

To find the advantage in using the inclined plane, divide the length of the plane by the height. In our example, the *mechanical advantage* would be ten divided by five, or two.

How You Can Experiment With an Inclined Plane

Take a pile of books — about one foot high — and put them on a table. Now attach a rubber band to the front of a toy car, rest your arm on the stack of books, and let the car hang by the rubber band. See how the weight of the car stretches the rubber band to a point where it might even break.

Now take a board, lean it against the books, and pull the car slowly up the inclined plane. You will see that the rubber band will not stretch as far as before, nor will it break.

If you have a spring balance, you can make the experiment even more scientific. Replace the rubber band with the spring balance and you will be able to check on the exact force needed to pull the weight of the car.

The Wedge

How is the wedge related to the inclined plane? When early man used a stone instrument to split the skin of an animal, we can be pretty sure that this stone was another of the six simple machines — the wedge. He didn't know at the time that he was using a "basic machine." He knew only that he was using something that enabled him to accomplish a task with less effort. The ancient Egyptians knew much more about the mechanical advantage of the wedge than primitive man. They

Splitting wood is made easier by using a wedge.

put two inclined planes together — back to back — and made a wedge. You could call that a movable inclined plane combination.

The wedge is used to overcome large resistance. You have probably seen the picture called "The Railsplitter," showing Abraham Lincoln using a wedge to split rails. The wedge is hammered into the log and splits it. Actually, all of our piercing tools, such as the ax, the needle, the knife, the carpenter's plane, and many others, are forms of the wedge.

How is the wedge used?

It is easy to understand the advantage of the wedge if you think what would happen if the knife or the needle were dull or the carpenter's plane had no blade. However, it is rather involved to figure out the exact mechanical advantage of the wedge as we did with the lever and the inclined plane. This is so because it is difficult to calculate the friction, and because the force applied to this machine is not steady as in the others. The force is intermittent; that is, it is applied in a series of uneven blows or stabs.

What is the advantage of using the wedge?

The Screw

You have been introduced to the inclined plane and to its cousin, the wedge. Now let's make the acquaintance of its other cousin, the screw. One of the best, and certainly one of the largest, examples of this simple machine is the staircase inside the Statue of Liberty in New York City. It is a steep spiral stairway which has 168 steps leading up to a balcony in the forehead of the statue. If you look at the illustration, you will see why we call it a giant screw, but can you see why the screw is related to the inclined plane?

How is the screw related to the inclined plane?

A screw is an inclined plane wrapped around a round object such as a pole or a cylinder.

Wood screws such as those shown

The staircase inside the statue resembles a screw.

next to the picture of the Statue of Liberty are generally used to hold things together — but larger forms of screws can be used for lighting. A pianist can raise the level of a piano stool simply by turning the seat. An automobile jack can raise a heavy car for changing a tire. And another type of jack can even lift a house from its site!

What is the pitch? When the screw is turned once, it advances a distance equal to the space between two grooves. We call this distance the pitch. The mechanical advantage of the screw is equal to the distance which the effort moves in one complete turn, divided by the pitch. When you see a large jackscrew in operation, you will be convinced that the jackscrew provides the greatest mechanical advantage of all the simple machines.

The principle of the screw has practical uses, including lifting houses and cars and adjusting piano stools.

22

How You Can Make a Screw Out of an Inclined Plane

You will use:

A square piece of paper, 3″ x 3″. Cut it so that you will have two inclined planes.
One round pencil
One colored pencil

Do this:

Color the long edge of the paper shaped like an inclined plane.

Wrap the paper about the pencil.

(Note: The colored edge should resemble a winding road or the colors of a barber pole.)

The inclined plane, of course, is still present. You can prove this by pushing a pencil point along the edge. It will climb the "road."

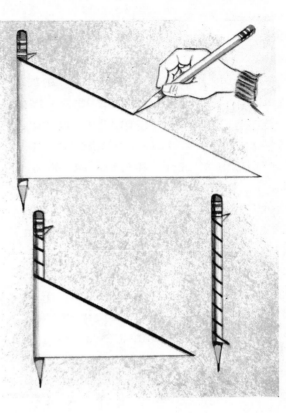

Why We Use Screws

You will use:

Four pieces of wood — from sides of an orange crate
One small nail
One small screw
A hammer
A screwdriver

Do this:

After placing two pieces of wood one on top of the other, hammer the nail in. Make sure they hold together.

Do the same for the other two pieces of wood — but use the screw and screwdriver.

Try to pry them apart.

Which pair is held together more securely? Why?

Which pair required more effort to put together? Why?

Was the extra effort you put into the pair being held together by the screw worth it?

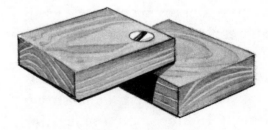

The Wheel

Primitive man made use of logs to move heavy objects.

Look around you, at home, in the street,

Why was the invention of the wheel important?

wherever you are or go, and just think what it would be like without the wheel. There would be no transportation at all, none of our complex machines and not even most of the simple ones. Even if machines are not all based on the wheel, most of them use it in one or another combination.

Just as we do not know who invented

What do we know about the development of the wheel?

the other simple machines, we do not know who invented the wheel. We do not even know when

and where it was used for the first time. We can assume that early man already had noticed that a round object moved more easily than one that was not round. We may assume that early man used logs to roll loads for short distances, but these were not really wheels.

We know that as far back as 4000 B.C., the Sumerians made use of the wheel. It was a heavy disk connected to an axle. It did not look at all like our wheel of today, but it was round and functioned as our wheel does.

The next improvement came when someone constructed a wheel with crossbars in an attempt to make it stronger.

The Egyptians made bronze wheels with spokes, which were quite strong and much lighter than the earlier wheels. They looked very much like a modern wheel. No doubt it already was

ROMAN CHARIOT

SUMERIAN WHEEL

ROMAN WHEEL

GALLIC WHE

DA VINCI WHEEL

a wheel rolling on its way to better and finer wheels to make work easier for all.

The Italian painter and inventor, Leonardo Da Vinci, who lived about five hundred years ago, improved the wheel further by making it lighter and stronger than it was.

The wheel in itself is not a machine, but

What makes the wheel a basic machine?

it becomes one when you combine it with an axle or another wheel. Actually, the axle is nothing but a second wheel, fastened rigidly to the first so that the wheel and axle turn together. Let's examine now the principles of the wheel and axle on a machine used by farmers years ago to raise water from the well — the windlass. The picture shows the larger wheel, attached to the axle, being four times the size of the axle; that is, the circumference of the wheel, or the distance around its outer edge, is four times that of the axle. One complete turn of the large wheel will turn the axle one time, since they are attached. If the circumference of the wheel is four feet, you will pull four feet of rope to turn the large wheel once, and wind one foot of rope on the axle. With a windlass, you can lift a bucket with one-fourth the effort.

You can also apply the laws of the lever to the wheel and axle. Going back to the windlass, let's say that if the big wheel makes one turn, it moves through a circle of four feet, and the bucket weighing forty pounds moves one foot up the well. Do you remember the law of the lever? The effort multiplied by the length of the effort arm equals the

The windlass is a combination of a wheel and an axle.

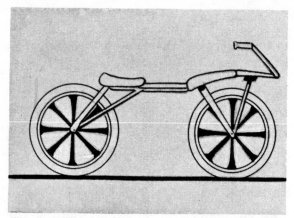

The very first bicycles constructed had no pedals.

resistance multiplied by the length of the resistance arm. In our example, 40 (the resistance) × 1 (the length of the resistance arm) equals 4 (the length of the effort arm) × 10. In other words, an effort of ten pounds raises a bucket of water weighing forty pounds — a mechanical advantage of four.

The idea that was behind the wheel and axle in the example of the windlass was also the idea behind the early bicycle. You probably remember from pictures that the front wheel with the pedals was very large, while the rear one was very small. When the rider turned the large wheel once with the foot pedal, the rear wheel turned many times. For example, suppose the small wheel were only one-quarter the size of the big wheel: When the rider turned the big wheel once with the pedal, the small wheel would turn four times. Such a bicycle would go four times faster than the same bicycle with two of the smaller wheels.

Later, pedals were connected to the large front wheel.

The pedals on today's bicycles turn the back wheel. The chain around this wheel turns the smaller, notched wheel.

You have seen, in the examples of the windlass and the early bicycle, how the wheel and axle work. Now let's examine the modern bicycle. We go easier and faster on the modern bicycle than people went on the early one, with its big front wheel and short rear wheel. Yet the front and rear wheels on the modern bicycle are the same size. It would seem as though what we explained before was wrong, but let's look closer.

How can wheels turn other wheels?

The inventor has attached a notched wheel and cranklike contraption with pedals to turn the wheel, to the front of the bicycle, just comfortably between the front and rear wheels. He also has provided a chain to fit exactly over the notches and a smaller notched wheel to fit the chain on the axle of the rear wheel. This small notched wheel turns with the rear wheel. When the large notched wheel with the chain and pedals is turned once, the rear small notched wheel to which the chain is attached turns many times, thus turning the large rear wheel with it. So we have a more complicated-looking machine, but the same basic principles obeying the same laws.

We do not have to go back to the windlass or the more complicated bicycle to study our problems. The doorknob is also a machine with a big wheel that turns a small wheel, and so is the eggbeater. If you examine the eggbeater, you will see that a wheel with teeth — or cogs, as they are called — engages and moves another wheel with cogs. In the modern bicycle this was done with a chain connecting the two wheels. In the eggbeater there is no connecting chain. Cogwheels that engage each other directly are called gears. Does this ring a bell in your mind? A machine as simple as the gear is an important part of a complicated machine like the automobile.

To make it a little easier for you to

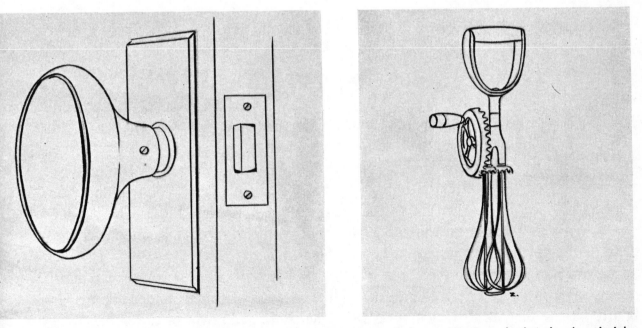

The doorknob and the eggbeater show two practical uses of the combination wheel and axle principle.

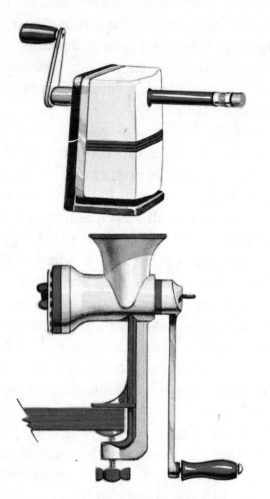

The meat-grinder above needs a longer effort arm.

recognize all the little and large machines that are basically wheel and axle, let us say that you can replace the large wheel by a crank, which acts like a wheel. Does this set the wheels turning? The pencil sharpener, the meat grinder, the crank that started the early automobiles . . . yes, all wheel and axle.

Let's see what we have learned — or

Why is a meat grinder handle longer than that of a pencil sharpener?

better, let's find out what we remember. Yes, indeed, the laws of the lever again!

As it is harder to grind the meat than to sharpen the soft wood of a pencil, we need the longer handle or effort arm to achieve our result with as little effort as possible.

Before we explain the one remaining simple basic machine — the pulley — let's first experiment a little with the wheel and axle.

How You Can Experiment With a Wheel

Take a board, drive a nail in the near

How can you reduce friction?

end, and attach to it a rubber band or — if you have one — a spring balance. Place a weight on the board. Now pull gently on the rubber band or the balance. If you have a balance, you can figure out the force of how many pounds you need to pull the board across the table. If you use a rubber band, you must simply try to

remember how far the rubber band stretches.

Now put three pencils under the board and pull again. You will find that you need much less force. The rubber band will not stretch as much as the first time.

Now try it again, putting some marbles instead of pencils under the board. The result again will be different.

You have proven that a rolling ob-

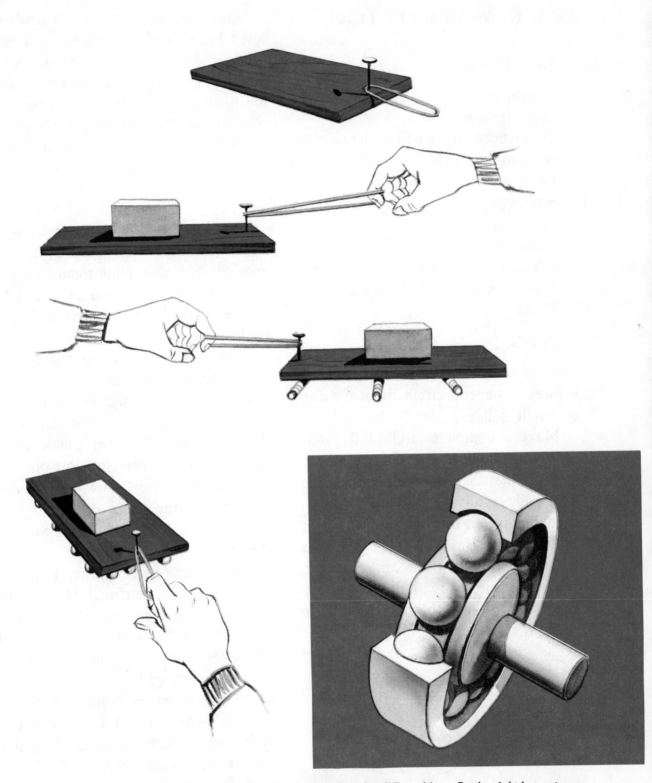

Wheels reduce friction so that the rolling object has less friction than the sliding object. On the right is a cutaway view of a wheel and axle showing the ball bearings (hardened steel balls) which are used to reduce friction.

ject has less friction than a sliding object. The difference between the pencils and the marbles is the same as that between the roller bearings used in heavy machinery and the ball bearings used in the wheels of an automobile.

How to Make a Lift Truck

You will use:

A cigar box
Paper fasteners
Two empty milk cartons (be sure to rinse them thoroughly with cold water)
One pencil with eraser
Scissors
Paper clip
Compass
A knife — or sharp cutter
Small box — about 1″ square
Pliers

Do this:

With the compass, measure off on a sheet of paper a circle about the size of a half dollar.

Make a complete circle and cut it out. Now you have a model of a wheel.

With the scissors, cut out one side of a milk carton. Using your model as a guide, cut out four wheels.

The paper fasteners will serve as axles. Bore a hole in the center of each wheel. Be sure to twist the paper fastener several times through the hole to make it ride easily.

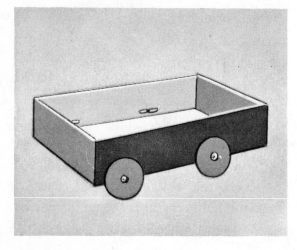

Since most cigar boxes are made of several thick layers of paper — or very thin wood — you will have no trouble making four holes for the axles. You are now ready to attach the wheels to your truck. Put the fasteners through the holes in the sides of the truck and open up the ends inside the box to secure the axles.

Try to roll it. *Hint:* If the wheels are not very sturdy, double them by making another set and stapling them together. If you are very ambitious, you can try making the truck with a cab and open back.

Now you are ready to put the lift wheel and axle into the truck.

Bore two holes through the front of the body of the truck. Put the pencil through them. With the pliers, cut a section of the paper clip. Put one end through the eraser. Now you have a handle for your wheel and axle. *Question:* Which is the wheel and which is the axle?

Tie a piece of strong thread securely to the center of the pencil. If you make a little notch in the pencil, the thread will not slip. By turning the handle of the wheel and axle, you can wind or unwind the thread.

Now you are ready for the track of your lift truck. Cut off one side of a milk carton and bend the two long sides over to face each other.

Cut another piece — the runner — one third the length of the track, but a little narrower to fit into it. Try to see if it fits and rides smoothly. Punch a hole at the top of this runner and tie the end of the thread into it.

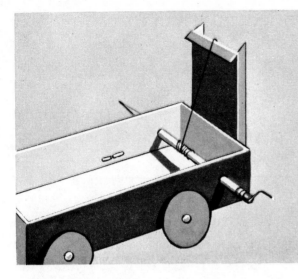

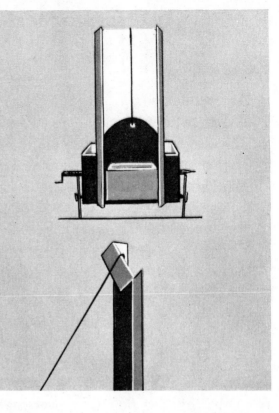

Attach the small box to the runner, either with staples or paper fasteners.

You are now ready to fasten the track and runner and box onto the front of the truck. Your stapler — or paper fastener — will do.

One more hint: Be sure to make a round edge for the thread to glide over the track.

Put some weight in the little box and wind up your wheel and axle. You are now ready to operate a lift truck.

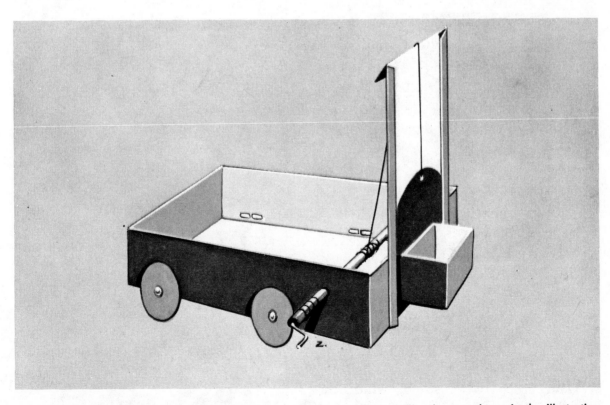

By following the directions, you should be able to construct a lift truck like the one shown in the illustration.

How to Make a Freight Elevator

You will use:

One wooden box
One large dowel stick
Wire hanger
Cord
Small box
Friction tape

Do this:

Remove the cover and base of the box. Make sure that the frame doesn't wobble by reinforcing it with angles. This is going to be a heavy-duty elevator, so it must be sturdy.

Bore two holes about two inches from the top and put the dowel shaft through.

Make a notch in the center of the dowel shaft and tie the cord to it.

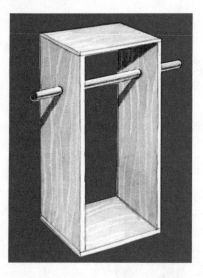

Now cut about six inches of the wire. Bend it into shape. It should be as rigid as possible, since it will serve as a handle for your wheel and axle.

Using the friction tape, wind the handle to the axle — many times, in a crisscross manner. Be sure it is tightly wound. Try it. Does it slip?

Of course, if you have an old handle that you can spare, use it. See if you can be an inventor.

Attach a box to serve as a car for your freight.

Wind the wheel and axle. Do you hear the dowel shaft squeak when the handle is turned? Why? Do you think a bit of grease or petroleum jelly might eliminate the noise? Try it.

If you want to do still better, try attaching a counterweight. Do this:

Place a stone weighing about half a pound in a small plastic bag and tie it with cord.

Instead of tying your cord to the notched dowel, attach the bag with the weight to the end of the cord and let it serve as the counterweight. As the freight car goes down, the counterweight will go up, and the other way round, too.

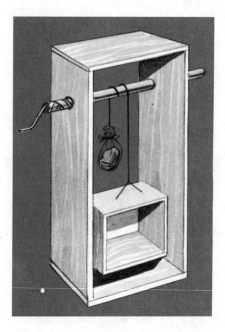

The Pulley

So far, we have made the acquaintance of five of the six basic machines. We have learned that machines, whether compound or basic, do not make less work. They enable man to do work with less effort. They make work easier. We have learned that machines are used for greater speed or for greater force — whichever suits the user best. A machine cannot give both increased force and increased speed at the same time. We have seen how the lever best illustrates the value of all machines, because every machine, in a sense, gives leverage (or *mechanical advantage,* as the scientists call it).

Why is the pulley often called a wheel with ropes?

Now it is time to meet the pulley, a basic machine that works very much like a first- or second-class lever.

The pulley enables you to raise and lower the flag.

It is a grooved wheel, or combination of wheels, used in combination with a rope or chain to lift heavy weights or, as we shall soon see, to change the direction of a force. We speak of a fixed pulley when the pulley is fastened by means of a hook to some support. A movable pulley is fastened to the weight being lifted.

33

The simplest type of pulley is the *single fixed pulley*. It

How does the single fixed pulley work?

sounds simple indeed, but did you ever try to figure out how, without this simple type of machine, you could raise or lower a flag without climbing to the top of the pole, or how the neighbors on the third floor could get the laundry on and off the clothesline?

Since the pulley is fixed — that is, attached to the top of the pole — and only the wheel turns, we do not get any mechanical advantage. We just change the direction of the force. We tie the flag to one end of the rope and pull the other end of the rope down, and — up goes the flag, to the top of the pole!

The mechanical advantage of the movable pulley is easy to
see, especially if you
think about what the
machine is used for
and if you remember your lessons from
the inclined plane and the lever. The
movable pulley and the combinations
we still have to learn about are used to
lift weights directly upward. We remember from the story of the inclined
plane how difficult this is. You arrange
your pulley, as *Figure 2* shows you,
fastening the rope on the far end and
fastening the pulley to the weight to be
lifted, and pulling on the other end.

**How is the
movable
pulley used?**

The mechanical advantage of the
pulley, like the advantage of all machines, may be obtained by dividing

the resistance by the effort. There is,
however, another method of determining the advantage, which applies only
to pulleys.

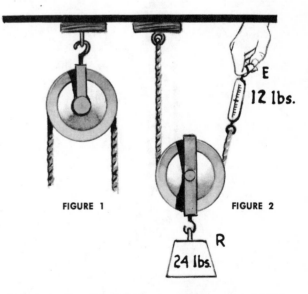

FIGURE 1   FIGURE 2

Single fixed pulley (left) and movable pulley (right)

We were interested with our arithmetic to find the mechanical advantage. But let us not forget that in general, in all our figuring, we can apply the law of the lever: Resistance multiplied by the distance it moves equals effort multiplied by the distance it moves. This means that for the pulley in *Figure 2,* two feet of rope must be pulled for every foot that the weight is raised $(24 \times 1 = 12 \times 2)$.

How does the combination of pulleys work? You have seen in *Figure 1* the single fixed pulley and in *Figure 2* the single movable pulley. *Figure 3* shows the combination of a fixed and a movable pulley, and *Figure 4* shows the combination of two fixed and two movable pulleys.

If you look closely, you will see that in *Figure 1,* the weight is supported by one section of the cord; in *Figure 2,* the weight is supported by two sections; in *Figure 3,* it is supported by three sections; and in *Figure 4,* by four sections. Now let's see how we can arrive at a special method of determining the mechanical advantage.

In *Figure 4,* we see on the spring balance that the pull to lift twenty-four pounds of weight is six pounds, so the mechanical advantage is $24 \div 6 = 4$. Now, remembering that the weight is supported by four sections of rope, we can see that each section actually carries only one-fourth of the load, or six pounds, and that — as you see registered on the spring balance — is the force exerted throughout the entire length of the rope. Thus, in the pulley — and only in the pulley — the mechanical advantage is equal to the number of strands of rope which support the weight.

Now that we have figured together the example for this combination of pulleys, try to do it without help for the other three examples.

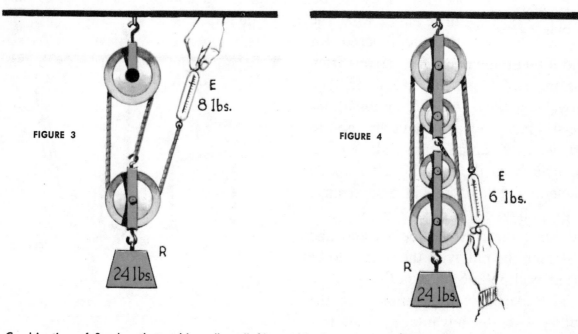

FIGURE 3

E
8 lbs.

R
24 lbs.

FIGURE 4

E
6 lbs.

R
24 lbs.

Combination of fixed and movable pulleys (left); combination of two fixed and two movable pulleys (right).

With the help of the pulleys, you can be "stronger."

How strong are you? Ask two of your friends who are taller and stronger than you to grasp a broomstick each and to stand several feet apart. Tie a clothesline to one of the sticks and wrap it several times around both sticks, as the picture shows. Ask them to hold tight to the sticks while you pull on the rope. You will see that you will pull the two sticks together and they will not be able to keep them apart. After you have accomplished this, explain to your friends how you did it. Here's a hint: you used a combination of pulleys.

How You Can Experiment With Pulleys

You will use:

Pulley, obtained from a five-and-ten-cent store for about 15¢
About five feet of cord
Small plastic bag
Four-pound weight (rock)

Spring scale
Broomstick or mop handle

Do this:

Put two chairs back to back, about three feet apart.

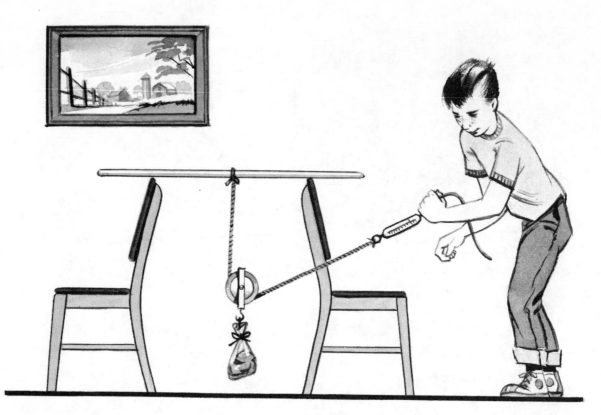

Place the broomstick across the top of the chairs.

Attach one end of the cord to the center of the stick.

Place the cord through the pulley so that the wheel rides freely, as if the cord were a track.

Place the weight in the bag and tie it.

Attach the weight to the pulley.

Attach the spring scale to the end of the cord and pull up.

This is your own movable pulley, and now you can check all the information that you have learned about it.

What does the scale read? As you know from the previous chapter, it should read two pounds. But it will read a little more than that because here, too, we have to overcome friction.

In the examples on the previous pages you saw a combination of a single fixed and a single movable pulley which was combined so that the mechanical advantage was three. If you do not remember it well, go back to *Figure 3* on page 36 for another look.

Now you should make your own combination, but hang it differently.

You will use:

Two pulleys
A short piece of cord
About five feet of cord
Plastic bag
Four-pound weight
Spring scale
Broomstick or mop handle

Do this:

Put two chairs back to back, about three feet apart.

Place the broomstick across the top of the chairs.

Attach one pulley to the center of the broomstick, using a short piece of cord. This will be the fixed pulley.

Tie one end of the five-foot piece of cord to the broomstick.

Pull this cord through the second, or movable, pulley and up through the first, or fixed, pulley.

Attach the free end of the cord to the spring scale.

Attach the weight, tied in the bag, to the movable pulley.

Pull and read the scale. Again it should read two pounds.

You will have to figure out whether the mechanical advantage is the same or different from your first pulley experiment — and whether it is the same or different from *Figure 3*. Whatever your results, you will find that it was easier to lift the weight — easier than in *Figure 3* and easier than in your own

previous experiment — because you were pulling down instead of up.

If you cannot buy pulleys, you can easily make your own. Cut off both wires of a wire clothes hanger at a distance of about seven inches from the hook. Bend the ends at right angles and slip both ends through an empty spool. Adjust the wires to allow the spool to turn freely and then bend the ends down to prevent the wires from spreading.

We have talked all this time about pulling a weight, pulling on the cord, and so forth. You might think, therefore, that the word *pulley* comes from the word "pull." But it doesn't. If you learn Greek, you will find that *pulley* comes from the Greek word *polós,* which means "axle."

Where does the word "pulley" come from?

39

The Sources of Energy

We have learned that in early times man relied entirely on muscular energy. The first step forward came when man learned to supplement his own muscular energy with that of animals. As man came to rely heavily on horse, ass, ox, and camel, he was slow to discover the uses of other natural sources of energy.

In the beginning of the book it was explained that energy is *the ability to do*

Windmill (above) and water mill (opposite page).

work. It was said that there are many forms of energy. Let's look a little more closely into this now, because energy and man's use of it is the main reason for the development of the machine.

If energy is the capacity to do work,

What are the different kinds of energy?

then water moving downhill has energy, the air that moves as wind has energy, and — as we know — we "have energy." What is this energy we have? Can we make it from nothing? Can we create energy? No. We always have to get it from somewhere. We have to get it from the moving air, the flowing water, or the oxidation of fuel. The oxidation of food provides muscular energy, the oxidation of fuel (when we burn coal or oil) provides energy for the steam engine, and so on.

Matter, as we will learn, may have two different kinds of energy, depending upon whether or not the energy is used or is just there, waiting to be used.

Water going over a waterfall, the weight of the pile driver coming down, steam expanding in an engine, are examples of active energy or, as the scientists call it, *kinetic energy*. The water in a reservoir, the weight of the pile driver resting on top of the machine, are not doing work, but they are in a position to do work. It is not active energy, but stored-up energy or, in the scientific term, *potential energy*.

Thus, kinetic energy is the energy matter has when it is in motion.

Potential energy is the energy matter has because of its position, its condition, or its chemical state.

How Man Harnessed the Forces of Nature

(1) *The windmill.* Man learned long ago to use a sail to catch the wind to drive a boat, but it was not longer than a thousand years ago that he attached the sail to a large wheel. As the wind blew, the wheel turned. This turned the axle to which the wheel was attached, and by using a combination of cogwheels, grindstones could be put in motion to grind grain into flour.

How has man harnessed the forces of Nature?

Later, in the Low Countries of Europe, where large sections of the land are below sea level, windmills were used to pump the water out of the fields. The early windmills had large canvas sails. Today, various improved types of windmills still are in use on farms for pumping water or for generating electricity on a small scale. Modern windmills have metal sails or blades and the wheel is much smaller and lighter. They are constructed in such a way that the wheel can turn freely and always catch the wind, no matter from which direction it blows.

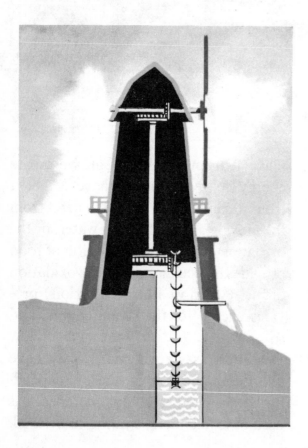

This is a cutaway view of a windmill showing the combination of wheel and axle and cogwheels.

(2) *The water wheel.* While the ancient civilizations of Mesopotamia used crude water wheels to help in the irrigation of the fields, not until the early Middle Ages did the people of Europe develop mills driven by the use of falling water.

In the course of time, several types of water wheels were developed, two of them closely associated with the early days of the American settlers and early American industry.

The *overshot wheel,* as the illustration shows, is turned by water falling upon the wheel from above.

The *undershot wheel* is operated by the force of running water striking the blades of the wheel from the bottom.

A third kind of water wheel was developed by the engineer Pelton and named for him. The *Pelton wheel* is turned by a strong stream of water directed against its blades from a nozzle. The advantage of the Pelton wheel is that it delivers more power than the overshot or undershot wheel and can be operated at a much greater speed.

The most efficient and useful type of water wheel today is the *turbine,* used to generate electricity. It consists of a large wheel with many blades, enclosed in a case or shell. Water piped from a great height first strikes a set of fixed blades attached to the casing, which causes the water to be directed with even greater force against the blades of the wheel and, in doing so, makes the wheel turn with great speed. While a great amount of energy is lost in overshot, undershot, and Pelton wheels, in the turbine the efficiency is more than 90% because of the casing.

From top to bottom: The undershot wheel, the overshot wheel, the Pelton wheel and the modern turbine.

43

How You Can Make a Model Water Wheel

You will use:

A cotton reel or a cork
10 pieces of wood or tin
A meat skewer or knitting needle

Do this:

Use the cork or the reel as the hub of the wheel.

Cut slots down the sides, at right angles to the ends, as shown in the illustration. Slide pieces of wood or tin into these slots.

Use the knitting needle or skewer as an axle.

Hang the wheel in a stand made from a metal clothes hanger.

The stream from a tap in your kitchen or bathroom will provide the water power to turn your water wheel.

This is your finished model water wheel ready for use.

We have seen now that man has learned

What are some other sources of energy?

to use water and wind as sources of energy to operate machines — more complicated machines than the six basic ones, but still machines that can easily

Energy can be changed from one form to another. Here, the boiler sets off the steam engine, which activates the dynamo, which lights a lamp, rings a bell and produces a chemical (electrolytic) reaction.

be traced back to the basic machines. However, only a small amount of the world's energy comes from wind and water. Most useful energy comes from fuels such as petroleum, gas, coal and wood. But only in the eighteenth century did man succeed in developing these sources of energy, and only quite recently did he start to develop the most powerful energy of all — atomic energy.

Wood and coal are burned in a furnace to boil water and produce steam that turns a steam turbine or steam engine; fuels that are liquids or gases can be burned in the combustion chambers of gasoline, diesel, or jet engines; and by "splitting the atom," atomic energy is released.

We have shown you and told you

What is an engine?

about the six basic machines and two early, more complicated machines. We have discussed what makes the machine do work. Let's finish now by explaining the difference between a machine and an engine.

While a machine is any device that

makes work easier by multiplying the force, changing the direction of the force, or increasing the speed with which the work is done, an engine is a device that is used to convert some form of energy — usually heat — into mechanical energy.

With this definition, we are near the end of our book, and at the beginning of the machine and atomic age.

Some Important Ideas for You to Remember

Machines have changed our ways of living in many ways — in getting food, making clothing, heating and lighting our homes, and our means of having fun. They have made work easier.

If we understand the simple machines, we can go on to understand the compound machines that are so much a part of our lives. These compound machines can be observed in the home, school, hardware store, toy store, factory, farm, garage and office.

Here are some important ideas about machines for you to remember:

1. If something has to be moved, we have to pull or push it. We use force to bring about movement.

2. We can use more force if we wish to pull or push faster.

3. The force that usually works against us when we push or pull along the ground is friction.

4. When we try to row a boat, we are resisted by the water.

5. Airplanes are resisted by the air through which they fly.

6. This force — resistance — can only be overcome by a greater force pushing against it. If the resistance is greater than the force, then we cannot move our object and no work is done.

7. Work is done only when something is moved.

Some Important Terms for You to Remember

BLOCK AND TACKLE: A combination of fixed and movable pulleys used for hoisting heavy objects.

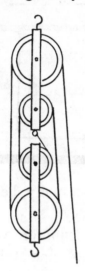

COMPOUND MACHINE: A machine consisting of two or more simple machines.

EFFICIENCY: The useful work done by a machine compared with the amount of work put in.

EFFORT: The force exerted on a machine.

ENERGY: The ability to do work.

ENGINE: A machine that changes energy from one form to another, usually mechanical energy.

FIRST-CLASS LEVER: A simple machine where the fulcrum is between the effort and the resistance, as in a seesaw.

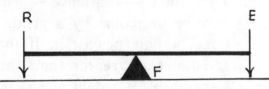

FOOT-POUND: Unit for measuring work done. One foot-pound is work done in lifting a pound one foot.

FORCE: A push or a pull, in order to move something or to stop something from moving.

FRICTION: The resistance that is caused when one object moves against another.

FULCRUM: The pivotal or "resting" point of a lever.

GEARS: Wheels with teeth or cogs that engage other gears.

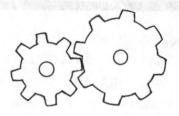

GRAVITY: The force of attraction between the center of the earth and objects on it or above it.

HORSEPOWER: Unit for measuring power—550 foot-pounds per second.

INCLINED PLANE: A simple machine consisting of a leaning surface along which objects may be pushed or pulled.

INERTIA: The tendency of a stationary object to remain at rest and a moving object to keep moving.

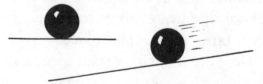

JACK: A machine used for lifting very heavy objects.

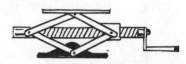

KILOWATT: One thousand watts.

KINETIC ENERGY: Energy of an object due to its motion, as a moving car.

LEVER: A simple machine upon which an effort is applied to gain force, speed or distance.

MACHINE: A device used to make work easier.

MECHANICAL ADVANTAGE: The gain in force obtained by using a machine.

PITCH: The distance between the threads of a screw.

POTENTIAL ENERGY: Energy of an object due to its position, as a rock at the edge of a cliff.

POWER: The rate of doing work, usually measured in watts or in horsepower.

PULLEY: A simple machine consisting of a grooved wheel over which a rope passes.

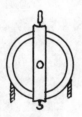

RESISTANCE: The force to be overcome by a machine.

SCREW: A simple machine consisting of an inclined plane wrapped around a cylinder.

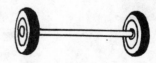

SECOND-CLASS LEVER: A simple machine where the resistance is between the effort and the fulcrum, as in an oar.

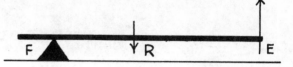

SIMPLE MACHINE: One of the six basic devices used to do work — inclined plane, lever, pulley, screw, wedge, and wheel and axle.

THIRD-CLASS LEVER: A simple machine where the effort is between the resistance and the fulcrum, as in a fishing rod.

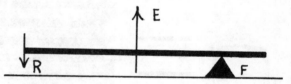

WATT: Unit for measuring electrical power.

WEDGE: A simple machine that is thick at one end and sloping to a thin edge at the other.

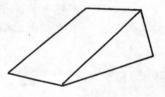

WHEEL AND AXLE: A simple machine consisting of a wheel or crank attached to an axle.

WORK: Applying force to move an object from one place to another.

Even the most complicated modern machines are combinations of two or more of the six basic machines described in this book. The picture above, for example, shows some of these basic machines. How many can you find?